STORIES FROM SCRIPTURE

ARCHIMANDRITE
VASILIOS BAKOYANNIS

STORIES FROM SCRIPTURE

Translated by

W. J. Lillie

ST. TIKHON'S SEMINARY PRESS
SOUTH CANAAN, PENNSYLVANIA 18459
2001

STORIES FROM SCRIPTURE

Copyright © 2001 by Archim. Vasilios Bakoyannis.
All rights reserved.

Published by
ST. TIKHON'S SEMINARY PRESS
P. O. BOX 130
South Canaan, Pennsylvania 18459
Printed in the United States of America

The icon on the front cover is used with the permission of Holy Transfiguration Monastery, Brookline, Massachusetts.

Library of Congress Cataloging-in-Publication Data

Bakoyannis, Vasilios, 1953-
[Histories apo ten Graphe. English]
Stories from Scripture / Vasilios Bakoyannis ; translated by W. J. Lillie.
p. cm.
ISBN 1-878997-64-5 (pbk.)
1. Bible stories, English--O.T. 2. Orthodox Eastern Church--Doctrines. I. Title.

BS558.G6 B3513 2001
221.9'505--dc21

00-068847

For Michael, Ekaterina, Maria and Andreas

"Search the Scriptures"
(John 5, 39)

Table of Contents

Prologue

The Old Testament is full of exciting stories. They are unique in their own way and full of drama, wisdom and truth. Stories such as these are presented in the pages that follow. Let us approach them with awe.

Chapter One: Ancestral Sin

All sorts of tribulations occur in this world of ours: injustices, murders, bloodshed and so on. We see them and hear about them every day. All of these evil sins, as tragic as they are, are placed in their proper perspective when compared with the first sin ever committed by man—the sin of the First-Created, Adam and Eve. Like the mother of a large family, that first sin gave birth to all the terrible tribulations that torment our world today. How did it happen?

The Glory of the First-Created

"And God saw that it was good" (Gen. 1, 8). That's what God said every time He finished one of His works, *"And He saw that it was good." God* saw—not man, not even an angel or an archangel—but God. His creation truly was good. It was a beautiful 'jewel' or an 'adornment'![1]

Now let's consider the *crown* of this creation, that is, mankind. Without exaggeration, the First-Created were not just simply

---

[1] In Greek, the word *kosmos* normally means "world" or occasionally "cosmos", but its literal and original meaning was "an adornment or ornament".

"people"—they were light! In particular, the Lord Himself tells us that in His Kingdom the righteous *"will shine like the sun" (Matt. 13, 43)*. Such will be their glory!

For the Church, this glory is the recovery of our ancient beauty. *"Refashion our ancient beauty"* writes the holy hymnographer, meaning the beauty and glory that the First-Created had. In other words, Adam and Eve shone in Paradise, they radiated as if they were the sun. They were bathed in divine light. How else could it have been, since they were creatures of God, who had only just emerged from His hands. And behold, people such as these fell into sin. And where did they fall—right in Paradise!

Envy

What would we say if some otherwise sensible person gave up his mansion for a hen-house? Wouldn't we be amazed at such stupidity? Now if that scandalizes us, imagine how outraged we should be by the fact that our glorious ancestors were cast out of Paradise into the thorns and thistles. How on earth did they manage to lose Paradise?

They were trapped. They were fooled by the envious devil: *"Deceived by the envy of the devil, he* (Adam) *partook of the food" (Burial*

Service). The devil once had the same glory as the First-Created. He, too, was light and dwelt in Paradise. But he envied the glory of God and lost his own glory. When he now looked upon the First-Created, with such glory and honor, he recalled his original beauty. He was consumed with envy. He did everything possible to get them out of Paradise. That, by the way, is what everybody does who has a heart like his. They see somebody, even one of their own, becoming successful and being praised and so on, and they begin to envy them. They'll do anything to "cut them down to size".

The Evil Plot

To get Adam and Eve out of Paradise was extremely difficult. This difficulty was increased because the devil wasn't dealing with ordinary people, but with those who were invested with divine light and the wisdom of God. He employed all his cunning in concocting his fiendish plan. This plan envisaged not appearing to the man (Adam), but to the woman (Eve). His plan was to try to trick her with "sweet-talk" and he would use the serpent as his instrument.

The Serpent

In our day, the very sound of the word "serpent" makes us shudder. But things were different back then. The serpent was familiar and friendly towards Adam and Eve, as indeed were all the animals and reptiles in Paradise. And not only that, but the serpent had something no other creature enjoyed: "*It was the cleverest of all the beasts upon the earth" (Gen. 3, 1)*. It was cleverer than all the other animals in Paradise. That is why the cunning devil used it as his tool to make sure that the work he wanted done would be done well.

Eve

The devil weighed up Adam and he weighed up Eve. He saw that the woman was more emotional. She could be moved and led more easily than the man. This is why he preferred to speak to Eve—and especially at a moment when she was alone. And notice one detail: the devil didn't bother Adam at all. He was confident in the trap he set for Eve.

The "Sweet-talk"

The most critical point in the whole affair was how to address wise and holy Eve. What exactly should he say in order to attain his goal? If a single wrong word escaped him, Eve would be in a position to know, or at least suspect, that all was not well. This is why the evil one was so careful here. Every word that emerged from his dirty mouth was carefully weighed and thought out. Let's take a closer look at his cunning.

God said to the First-Created: "*You are forbidden to eat the fruit of* ***one*** *tree in Paradise*" *(Gen. 2, 17)*. The devil asks Eve exactly the opposite: *"Why has God forbidden you to eat the fruit of* ***any*** *tree?" (Gen. 3, 1)*. The devil knew what he was doing here. With the question *"Why has God . . ."* he shows that, supposedly, he cares about Eve and is interested in her. In other words, he appears as her protector *(St. John Chrysostom, Homily 16, On Genesis)*. That in itself should have been enough to infuriate Eve and make her say to the devil: *"How dare you utter such things against my Creator and God?"* But Eve was trapped. She was "hooked" by the interest shown by the devil. She was in his confidence and thus she started a discussion with the devil!

She told him: "*We can eat of the fruit of all the trees. It's only the fruit of the one that's in the middle of Paradise that we can't eat, lest we die" (Gen. 3, 2-3).* The cunning devil, full of guile, answered: *"No, you won't die. He forbade you to eat it because He knew that on the day you did so, your eyes would open. You would be like Him. You would know good from evil" (Gen. 3, 5).*[2] He said nothing else to her, nothing except those few words.

There are two points worth noting here. First, God tells the First-Created that if they eat of the fruit of the forbidden tree, they will

---

[2] The devil didn't tell Eve she'd become malicious and cunning, but that she'd be like God, knowing good from evil. In other words, he told her something good and useful, and that's how he tricked her. This is how the devil tricks (deceives) his victims. He drives them towards sin for supposedly good reasons. The thief steals for a good purpose (to provide for his family, for example), the young man is a philanderer out of love, a spouse gets a divorce for the good of everyone concerned, terrorists carry out murders for the good of the cause and so on. "*The road to Hell is strewn with good intentions.*" People do evil with a good purpose because they are, by nature, good. We can't do evil without relating it to good. Otherwise it would come into conflict with our nature. People are good by nature because that's the way the Good Lord has made us. In other words, like father (God), like son (people). If God is good by nature, people are good by nature, too.

die, but again the devil tells Eve exactly the opposite: *"You will be like God" (Gen. 3, 5).* They will become **gods** and will **never** die. He had to find something to excite the woman's vanity, and he did.

Second, it was the devil's aim to get the First-Created out of Paradise, but he didn't reveal this to Eve. He didn't tell her bluntly and clearly, *"You have got to get out of Paradise."* He knew that if he did so, he would fail miserably. This is why he didn't give a hint of his treacherous and underhand purpose. The First-Created were left with the impression that they would remain in Paradise, and, moreover, as gods![3] Furthermore, they

---

[3] The devil is still the same today, perhaps even worse. He tries to employ the same deceit he used against the First-Created against all Christians who are in Paradise, that is, in the Church. In order to get them to lose their souls, he doesn't say bluntly and clearly, *"Leave Christ and go to Hell"* because that would be counter-productive. *"Even now he does not say 'Forsake Christ', because he knows he is a liar and would not be believed" (Saint John Chrysostom, On Destiny and Providence, 2).* This is why he tries to trap us in a different way. He allows us to believe in Christ, to remain within the Church, but he tries to get us involved with anything and everything else other than **how to save our souls!** He tries to deceive us in a very treacherous way, so that we don't suspect anything and thus he draws us away from the

were led to believe that God was somehow afraid (!) that they would become like Him. Eve believed the "sweet-talk" (that is, the blasphemies) of the devil and thus brought ruin on the whole world.

The Great Tragedy

"And the woman saw that the tree was good to eat" (Gen. 3, 6). The forbidden tree wasn't any different from the other trees in Paradise. There wasn't anything special about it to attract particular attention. Yet now Eve longed after it. Why? Hadn't she ever seen it before?

Of course she had, but before she'd been indifferent to it and her thoughts didn't keep going back to it. Now, under the influence of the devil, she saw it in a different light. She couldn't dismiss it from her thoughts. She kept gazing at it. Her imagination ran riot.[4] Finally she decided to eat from its fruit.

Kingdom of God: *"Without their knowledge he snatches their eternal inheritance" (Saint John Chrysostom, ibid.).* This should give all of us food for thought. The enemy doesn't make any exceptions.

[4] The sin didn't start from the outside, from the fruit, but from the inside, from the *thought*. It was the *thought* that brought the sin, not the fruit in itself. In other words, "things" do not make people sin (such as money, drink, the flesh and so on); it is the evil

Somewhere nearby was her husband. If she'd had any sense, she'd have shared her thoughts with him, discussed it, asked his opinion. And yet, she snubbed him. She was adamant in her own deluded mind that she was absolutely right. What need did she have of his opinion?

So she took the first step. Her sensitive conscience recoiled. Drunk as she was on vanity, she paid no attention. She continued. She reached the forbidden tree, grabbed a fruit and gobbled it down.

She tasted the bitter fruit of sin and immediately she felt such intense regret and guilt! Despite this, she wanted to involve her husband as well. She was upset as she approached him. Adam now saw a different Eve. He'd never seen his wife like this before. Despite this, he gave it no thought. He, too, ate of the fruit of the forbidden tree.

So it wasn't only Eve who sinned, but Adam as well. What is more, this sin took place right in the middle of Paradise! Some people are puzzled by this and ask: *"Since God knew that the First-Created would fall, why did He even create them?"* Did God make a mistake by creating them?

---

thought, that is, the *inclination* which leads people to sin.

What blasphemy! What should God have done, not even create Adam and Eve in the first place? Or, perhaps because He is good, wouldn't it have been better to prevent them from sinning at all? But then He'd have deprived them of the freedom that He himself had given them.

God did not create them so that they would sin, but so that they would become perfect. The fact that they sinned is *their* responsibility, not that of God the Creator.

After the Fall: Nakedness and Shame

"Then the eyes of both were opened, and they realized that they were naked" (Gen. 3, 7). They had been naked before *(Gen. 2, 25).* How was it that they discovered their nakedness only now? Previously, their naked bodies had been clad in divine light. When they sinned, however, they lost this light, this immaterial garment. In other words, their souls were laid bare. When the soul is naked, so is the body.

They saw their naked bodies and were ashamed: *"And they sewed fig leaves and made themselves aprons."* As man and wife, they were ashamed to look at each other. Their shame automatically brought concealment with it. They instinctively covered up the "unmentionable" parts of their bodies, thus showing that the "mind" of the sinner revolves around this area.

Call to Repentance

Our Merciful God *"moved heaven and earth"* to bring them to repentance, with the aim of keeping them in Paradise. He pretended to be ignorant of events in the hope that they'd be moved to confess their sin. Three times (twice with Adam and once with Eve) he called them discreetly to repent, but three times they refused the invitation. That's how perverse they became!

The first call: *"Adam, where are you?" (Gen. 3, 9).* God speaks with great discretion. He does not say: *"What on earth have you done, you sinner?"* Rather, he asks, *"Adam, where are you."* He calls him by name and without blaming him for what he's done. He does this for two reasons.

First, Adam was already wounded by the arrow of sin. In other words, he was in a bad psychological state. The Good Lord, like a wise mentor, doesn't want to chafe the wound by rebuking him.

Second, these three words, *"Where are you?"* may mean nothing to us. But they meant a great deal to the guilty Adam. They made him think about his sin and thus opened the way to repentance. Knowing how difficult it was for Adam (and for every sinner) to acknowledge his sin, God tried in this way to give him the courage to open his heart.

But Adam (who had shone like the sun!) was unmoved. Not only that, but he tried to deceive God with a little lie, *"I heard Your voice and was afraid. I'm naked and I hid" (Gen. 3, 10).* How incredibly perverse! God calls him to repent yet he runs away to hide from God, Who is everywhere present.[5] Sin now made him act ridiculous and childish.

The second call: Although our merciful God saw that Adam was deliberately trying to make a fool of Him, He continued to speak calmly and affectionately to him. His purpose was to soften Adam's soul, not to harden it; to save the sinner, not to scourge him.

---

[5] As long as Adam was pure, he had no problem with God. He would run to Him, longing to see Him. Now that he was stained by sin, however, he felt too ashamed and afraid to gaze upon God. He ran away to hide. That means that it's not God's fault that people are estranged from Him, but the fault of sin. It's not the Church's fault that people (especially the young) stay away from her, but the fault of sin. It's not the priests' fault that people don't go to confession, but the shame and uncleanliness of sin.

"Who told you that you were naked? Did you eat from the tree I forbade you to eat of?" Adam was now cornered. What was he to say, that he hadn't eaten? God knows everything. Adam confessed indirectly that he had eaten, but without showing any repentance. He said to God: *"The woman that* ***You gave me*** *gave me it to eat." "That You gave me,"* he said. It's as if he were saying: *"It's all Your fault, and my wife's, but not mine. I am innocent!"*

The third call: Eve was nervously following this critical discussion. She could see that any time now it would be her turn to be "interrogated". So she worked out in her mind the answer she would give to God. The Good Lord approached her. He spoke to her with affection and discretion, with the hope that she would respond: *"Why did you do this?"* And she told Him bluntly: *"The serpent deceived me."*

Adam referred God to Eve, and she referred Him to the serpent. Out of goodness and mercy and in the hope that they would repent, the Lord and God of All deigned to be bounced about like a ball by His own creatures. But neither Adam nor Eve repented, even though they had seen God and experienced life in Paradise.

The Mouse

One of Aesop's fables relates how there was once a cat that decided to get married. The time for the wedding had arrived, and so did the guests. The cat was all dressed up for the wedding and very pleased with herself. Suddenly, she smelt a mouse. She forgot about everything and everybody. She zeroed in on the mouse in a corner. The bewildered mouse ran about from pillar to post, with the cat (bride) chasing after it. The wedding had to be called off.

Something similar also happened with the First-Created. Their souls had contracted a marriage with the Heavenly Bridegroom, but they were seduced by love of pleasure (that is, eating the forbidden fruit). They made fools of themselves, and their wedding, too, had to be called off. Even today, it seems as if people have not changed much from the same shortcomings of the First-Created.

Points to Ponder

Adam sinned, although he lived in a world that knew no sin. He also (we repeat) saw God. Lucifer also sinned, though he had no body (carnal desires), though he had no such temptation to trouble him and though he had stood at the throne of God, continuously illumined.

Think how easy it is for us, who are full of passions and sin, to sin in this sinful world. Yet God asks us **not** to sin, even in our thoughts! *"Adam, where are you?"* That is how the Lord sought sinful Adam, calling him to repentance. Indeed, God wants to save **all** people *(cf. 1 Tim. 2, 4)*.

So, just as He was concerned about the salvation of the First-Created, He is also concerned about the salvation of every one of His lost sheep. He seeks them and *"calls them by name."*

The Good God also calls us. He invites us to be close to Him and calls us by name, *"Where are you?"*

So what are we going to do? Imitate the First-Created, who ran away to hide, mocking the Lord?

Chapter Two: Cain

Adam had already tasted the first bitter fruits of his action. Nature had become wild. From having been tame, the animals also became wild. The earth was filled with thorns and thistles. Evil even occurred within his own home. His son Cain murdered his brother Abel in cold blood. One brother killed the other! Adam in his misery was unable to swallow the fact that the devil had deceived him and that everything could have been turned upside down so quickly.

The Sacrifice

Cain was a farmer and Abel a shepherd. One day, both of them offered a sacrifice to God. Who taught them (asks Saint John Chrysostom) to offer sacrifice to God? It was their conscience! But what each of them offered depended on their mood and their intentions *(Homily 18, On Genesis)*. Cain offered what came to hand: *"of the fruits of the earth" (Gen. 4, 3)*. In essence, it was a chore for him and he couldn't wait to be finished. What Abel did for God, on the other hand, he did with his heart. This is why he offered Him the best he had: *"of the first-born of his sheep and of their fat" (Gen. 4, 4).* The result of this was that God accepted the sacrifice of Abel, but rejected that of Cain *(Gen. 4, 4-5).*

Envy and Murder

The virus of envy is peculiar in one way: it doesn't strike just anywhere, but rather among colleagues, friends, relations and even brothers. In other words, as persons we won't feel any envy at the success of somebody we have never heard of, but we will if someone close to us does well! In this case, Cain envies Abel because he's his brother and because God accepted his sacrifice.

"Cain was very angry" (Gen. 4, 5). Instead of rejoicing at having such a good brother, he was consumed with anger because of his jealousy! His mind and heart were inundated by wild thoughts. He had to do something . . .

The Good Lord Who reads our hearts knew that His servant was boiling over and ready to burst apart. In an effort to prevent the worst, He advised him: *"Why are you sad and morose? Don't you know that if you offer gifts to God and they are not good gifts then that is a sin?" (cf. Gen. 4, 6-7).* It was as if God was saying, *"Put a stop to this; don't go on with it; calm down."*

Cain took no notice of God's constant appeals. He disdained them, not because he *could not* heed them, but because he refused to do so *(Saint John Chrysostom, Homily 18, On Genesis)*. That's when everything started going downhill . . .

"Let's go to the plain," he said to his brother. The unsuspecting Abel agreed to his suggestion and off they set. Cain knew that they were spending their last moments together as brothers and that soon his brother would no longer be with him. Even though he knew that he would soon be dead, he *still* wasn't moved. Envy had killed his soul, which is why he was going to kill his brother.

They reached the plain. Cain began to strike his brother. Abel was caught off guard. No doubt he asked for an explanation, maybe even for forgiveness for inadvertently hurting Cain. He would certainly have entreated to stop this evil.

But Cain, deadened by the fatal virus of envy, was unmoved and unfeeling in the face of the cries of his dying brother. He continued to strike him. This is what submission to passion brings. He saw the blood flowing on the earth, he heard his brother's groans, but was still unmoved. He went on and on until he finished him off. Then he disappeared.

The Merciful God

Of course God could have intervened at the moment when Cain was killing Abel. He could have immobilized him and thus prevented the evil from occurring. But He didn't. He remained a spectator to the crime, because He wants us to fight against the passions and exercise virtue of our own accord. Otherwise virtue isn't virtue; it is blackmail.

No sooner had Cain killed his brother than God appeared to him. He does so not in order to chastise him and to "bawl him out" as we might have done, because of our passions. Rather, God tried to lead him along the road to repentance.

Just as He had spoken caringly and discreetly to Adam the sinner, so now the Lord God spoke in the same way to Cain the murderer. He didn't say: *"You're a murderer! You killed your brother,"* because that would have wounded him and it would have made the job of repentance more difficult. Instead, He asked him: *"Where is your brother?"*

Cain replied to God's tactfully phrased question with a lie: *"I don't know!"* Adam, too, had replied to the question: *"Where are you?"* with a lie. But just as God wasn't angered by the deceit of Adam, so now He remained calm in the face of similar deceit on the part of Cain the murderer.

Again, He asked discreetly: *"What have you done? The voice of your brother's blood is crying out to me from the earth."* He doesn't say directly: *"You killed your brother,"* but *"What have you done?"* He doesn't say, *"Your brother, whom* **you** *killed,"* but *"your brother's blood is crying out."*

What kindness and discretion on the part of God! Here, too, the aim was not to condemn Cain but to save him by bringing him to repentance. But just as Adam and Eve did not repent, neither did Cain. God Himself struggled to bring all three of them to repentance, yet He could not! Repentance is a great mystery indeed.

Punishment and Contrition

Punishment: Despite the best efforts of the Merciful Lord, Cain still refused to repent. The moment came for him to reap the rewards of his actions. God announced his punishment: "*You are now cursed from the earth, which has opened its mouth to receive your brother's blood from your hand. When you till the ground, it shall no longer yield its strength to you. A fugitive and a vagabond you shall be on the earth" (Gen. 4, 11-12).*

Contrition: Cain heard his terrible punishment from the mouth of the Lord and finally came to his senses! He confessed his sin at once: *"What I have done is beyond the bounds of divine forgiveness (Gen. 4, 13, LXX).* In other words, he felt himself unworthy of divine forgiveness. What terrible desolation!

Unfortunately for Cain, it was too late. *"Behold,"* writes Saint John Chrysostom, *"Cain confessed with total sincerity. But there was no benefit at all. His confession was too late. He should have confessed while there was still time."*

"The same thing (he continues) *will happen to each of us on the dread Judgment Day. When we then see the horrible tortures we, too, will repent of our sins. But on that day, our confession will be too late and invalid. So please, let us repent now while we are still alive" (Homily 19, On Genesis).*

Chapter Three: The Flood

Evil spread throughout the face of the earth without resistance. It gushed in like a river, covering the whole of it. The world was deluged with evil. There was a "flood" of evil. This had to happen in order for evil to cease and for society to be cleansed. And that's what happened . . .

The Degenerate World

"Then the Lord saw that the wicked actions of men were multiplied on the earth and that every one of them was intentionally brooding over evil in his heart every day" (Gen. 6, 5).

"The wicked actions of men were multiplied." It doesn't say that evil was multiplied, but that the evil actions of men were multiplied. Wherever there is wantonness, worldly pleasure and excessive license (teaches Saint John Chrysostom) many other passions are also born. Wantonness then becomes a primary source from which untold other evils flow *(Homily 23, On Genesis).*

"Every one of them was intentionally brooding over evil in his heart." Evil was being done (according to Saint John Chrysostom) not only by the young, but also by the old; not only by men, but also by women; not only

by the enslaved, but also by the free; not only by the poor, but also by the rich. They did not sin out of carelessness or because they were led astray—they did it intentionally. They were professionals at it! In other words, the thing that they were really interested in was how best to do evil. The saving thought of repentance never crossed their minds.

They sinned *"every day"* throughout their whole lives. And in those days people lived for six hundred, seven hundred, even eight hundred years. For all those years, they sinned continually. Sin was their permanent occupation. That's the kind of world Noah lived in.

Noah

Noah was the son of Lamech and a great-great-grandson of Adam. He lived not long after the expulsion from paradise of his forefather Adam. But despite the fact that he lived in a depraved world, he himself exuded virtue.

"And Noah lived five hundred years and sired three sons, Shem, Ham and Japheth" (*Gen. 5, 32*). Saint John Chrysostom comments that it is not without reason that Holy Scripture tells us that Noah lived five hundred years before he had any children. This

is done in order to show, in an indirect way, the measure of his restraint. In other words, while everyone else around him were all foaming at the mouth with carnal desires, Noah was chaste until the age of five hundred. He controlled the unruly flesh for so long and to such a degree that he not only avoided illicit sex outside of marriage, but he did not even indulge in legitimate sexual relations *(cf. Saint John Chrysostom, Homily 24, On Genesis)*. Remember, Noah lived before Christ and in a most degenerate society.

Living in chastity in such a world, Noah stuck out like a sore thumb. From neighbors, friends and relatives he heard mocking comments on an everyday basis—for five hundred years! He was a laughing-stock, a real "weirdo".

He never received a good word of advice from any fellow man, nor was there anyone to be found to encourage him in the struggle against the flesh. Instead, he was thrashed and whipped around as if by wild waves. But he was not disheartened. He ploughed his course calmly across the stormy sea, like a mighty athlete for virtue.

" . . . being perfect in his generation" (Gen. 6, 9). Virginity is of great value, and especially when it is preserved among people living

wantonly. So Noah's chastity was even more precious, because it had been maintained for nearly five hundred years—living in a virtual "brothel"!

"Noah was a righteous man" (Gen. 6, 9). In the Scriptures, a person is righteous when he applies all the statutes and commandments of God. In other words, Noah wasn't merely chaste, but conscientiously prudent in all things. He was *"perfect in his generation,"* in a society that bore a deadly hatred for virtue. His life was so virtuous that he earned the praise of the Lord Himself: *"Noah was well-pleasing to God" (Gen. 6, 10, LXX).*

How did he manage this? How on earth did he manage to reach such heights in all that chaos and deep darkness? Why wasn't he too overcome by the stifling pressure brought to bear on him continuously by the depraved mob? *"Because,"* replies Saint John Chrysostom, *"his mind was permanently centered on God and he was not in the least concerned what others said about him. The example of Noah shows us that nothing can hinder people who want to be chaste, to be watchful and to care excessively for their salvation. So let no one blame others. Let no one think that others are responsible, but let them rather ascribe it to their own indifference" (Homily 23, On Genesis).*

God's Warning

The first warning: "*Then the Lord saw that the wicked actions of men were multiplied*" (*Gen. 6, 5*). Was it only then that God saw how people's wicked actions had increased? Didn't He know before? Of course He did!

Saint John Chrysostom, however, points out that the Scriptures want to teach us that people persisted in sin despite the fact that God was long-suffering. Not only that, but they became even worse: "*The wicked actions of men were multiplied.*"

"*And He grieved that He had made man upon the earth" (Gen. 6, 6).* The long-suffering God, seeing His creatures floundering in the cesspit of sin, thought of the day when He had created them. Saint John Chrysostom puts these words into the mouth of God: "*Is this really what I put men on earth for? To fall so dangerously low? To become the cause of his own perdition? No. From the beginning I have held mankind in particular honor and have shown special attention toward man so that they should not be lost. But because they have not made good use of My love, 'I shall have to destroy mankind whom I have created from the face of the earth, for I am sorry that I have made them' (Gen. 6, 7);" (cf. Homily 22, On Genesis).*

"And their days shall be a hundred and twenty years" (Gen. 6, 3). There are two important details worth noting here. Firstly, even though people had fallen so low, the Merciful Lord was in no hurry to wipe them off the face of the earth. God was even willing to wait another hundred and twenty years!

Secondly, He warned them, hoping that they would come to their senses, wake up, repent and escape punishment. And so as not to distress them, He put time at their disposal—a hundred and twenty years!

The thief on Christ's right didn't need more than a moment to repent. Given a hundred and twenty years, people have time not only to repent, but to become even higher than the angels!

The second warning: the construction of the ark. *"And the Lord said: 'The time of every man has approached me'."* (*Gen. 6, 13*). God announced to His friend Noah His great decision: *"Mankind's end has arrived."* And He (God!) gave His reasons: " . . . *for the earth has been filled with unrighteousness" (Gen. 6, 13).* The earth was full of evil. Things had gone too far. They could not continue like this. God was going to flood the whole world with water, so that nothing should remain alive. Every last thing would be killed. He promised, however, that He would save Noah. He told him to build an ark for himself, his wife and his children *(Gen. 6, 14-18).*

Noah obeyed. He hired workers. They cut timber from the forest, transferred it and set up a "ship-yard". With the primitive methods available to them at the time, they built a gigantic boat . . . on land! It took them no less than one hundred years *(cf. Gen. 7, 6).*

The construction aroused everyone's curiosity. They all wanted to know what was going on, so Noah seized the opportunity to preach a sermon on repentance. And the workers, too, when they were striking the timber every day, were also striking **consciences** (including their own), in order to awaken them. Noah and his workers, for a hundred years, were sounding the call to repentance.

And not a single person repented! They cared only for the "dolce vita", that is, the "sweet life", a life of indolence and self-indulgence. They had their own ideas. No doubt they said things like: *"Noah has lost his mind! Here he is, building a boat where there isn't any sea."* Or perhaps, *"Noah pretended to be so religious and here he is getting involved with business enterprises."*

The third warning: the gathering of the animals. Already one hundred years had passed. The depraved people didn't show the slightest inclination to repent. So our Merciful God cut short the time, hoping that they would finally wake up. He made the remaining twenty years only seven days! *(Gen. 7, 4).*

He gave orders that Noah, his family and every kind of bird and animal should embark *(Gen. 7, 1-3).* Before, people saw the workers making the ark and said whatever it was they said. Now they saw Noah and his family, the animals, the birds all inside the ark for seven days, waiting! *(Gen. 7, 10).* And *still* they were unmoved.

They were so hard-hearted and deluded by their passions. They were trapped by their own arguments and their own point of view. They thought that they were the ones who were correct. It didn't even occur to them that they might be mistaken in their judgment. They were under the illusion that Noah was the one who was deluded and that they were on the strait and narrow.

The Flood

Suddenly, what they least expected happened —their own destruction: *"The flood-gates of heaven opened" (Gen. 7, 10).* Torrential rain fell. The water came down in sheets. Nor was that all: *"All the fountains of the abyss cracked open" (Gen. 7, 11).* All the underground springs burst forth. The earth and the heavens vented their wrath. For forty whole days and nights with no let-up, the waters poured relentlessly onto the earth.

What a nightmare for the unrepentant, seeing rivers of water welling out of the ground before them and also falling upon their heads, for so many days and nights.

What pain they must have felt when they saw their houses, crops and flocks washed away! What terror must have seized them when they realized that they had come to the end of the road! Like lost souls they must have run around trying to find anything to cling on to in order not to drown. No doubt they shouted for help as well, but who was there to help them?

What suffering did they experience when they saw parents, children, friends and relatives overwhelmed before their very eyes? What agony did they feel when they saw no chance of the weather clearing to blue skies?

Perhaps then they remembered Noah and the truth he had been trying to tell them.

Some may have managed to climb up into high trees. But the unheard of rain showed no signs of letting up. So the level of the waters rose until they, too, were drowned. Even those who managed to get away high up into the mountains were only fooling themselves. The waters reached them even up there. They covered all the highest summits *(Gen. 7, 20)*. For a hundred and fifty days, everything was covered with water *(Gen. 7, 24)*.

The earth had become one great boundless ocean. Everyone drowned, even those who had built the Ark. God gave them one hundred years in which to repent, yet they mocked His kindness.

The Ark floated on the stormy waters from November when the deluge began, until April when the waters began to recede *(Gen. 8, 3)*. For five whole months it was tossed back and forth.

There was a great danger of it being swallowed up by the waves or striking a reef and running aground. Yet the survivors were all safe and sound, and they finally landed on

Mount Ararat,[6] *(Gen. 8, 4)* as if they had an experienced, skilled and patient captain in charge, as indeed was the case.

Noah entered the Ark on the twenty-second day of the second month (that is, November, cf. *Gen. 7, 11)* and left on the twenty-seventh day of the second month (cf. *Gen. 8, 14)* the next year, after the earth had dried. For a whole year they were confined to the Ark, without knowing where they were or where they would end up.

There weren't any generators to produce light in the Ark, so for a whole year Noah was in darkness. And he would have grown accustomed to the many and different sounds he heard that were made by the animals he had brought with him. The Ark must have reeked from their accumulated dung.

Inside the Ark, Noah would have known, when the storm broke, that everyone outside would be lost, including the workers who had labored a hundred years with him, as well as

---

6 Saint John Chrysostom tells us that even in his own days, the remnant of the Ark was known to be found on Ararat: "*Have you heard about the Flood and that total destruction? Remains of it (the Ark) are still to be found to this day, for our remembrance.*" *(On Perfect Love, 7).* Today it has been shown scientifically that the Flood was a historical event. This is further proof that the Bible is to be trusted as a historical record.

his friends and relatives with whom he had lived for nearly six hundred years. No doubt he would have heard their despairing cries. What pain for gentle Noah!

Despite living in such dramatic conditions, Noah did not lose heart, he did not despair and he did not panic. He surrendered himself entirely to God. He showed complete trust in Him. In return for this confidence, the Lord of All did not abandon him. On the contrary, He was with him all the time. He supported, strengthened and fortified him.

Indeed, Noah felt this. That's why no sooner had he stepped onto dry land than he offered a sacrifice to God as proof of his gratitude for His great support *(Gen. 8, 20)*.

Conclusion

The people who were drowned in the Flood lived before Christ. Not only that, but the Ten Commandments still had not been given to Moses. In other words, they lived in deep darkness. Despite that, they were punished by death for their sins, particularly those of the flesh. Why? Because they did not even struggle. They made no effort to overcome their passions and sin. If they had tried, they would have triumphed, as did Noah.

This means that if we too do not struggle against our passions and sin, and just give in without a fight, we too will be punished. God may be patient with us, even for a long time, as He did back then. Ultimately, however, the price will have to be paid.

It is interesting to note that the depraved people in the time of Noah had a change of heart only after the Flood broke, not before. This brings to mind one of Aesop's fables. The story is that once there was a little goat on the roof of a two-story house. It sees a wolf on the street below and starts berating it in the strongest terms for eating the flocks of the poor. *"Come down here, if you want to talk,"* replies the wolf. If the goat had actually confronted the wolf at such close distance, we may be sure that the first thing it would have done would have been to ask for forgiveness for its tirade and to beg for its life.

Well, the populace in Noah's time (as well as in our own), as long as they were in no danger, spoke like the little goat up on the roof. When they found themselves in the jaws of death, they repented and cried for help.

By then, unfortunately for them, it was too late.

CHAPTER FOUR: ABRAHAM

Christ calls paradise *"the bosom of Abraham" (Luke 16, 22)*. This means that there was something special about Abraham, which attracted even Christ Himself. It wasn't just that he had a hospitable heart, which is why we talk about the "hospitality of Abraham". He had something incomparably superior; he had total self-denial for the sake of God. He left his house and his own land for the sake of God. Even more astonishing, he was willing to sacrifice his only son for His sake!

If we analyze this "self-renunciation" on the part of Abraham, we find certain virtues that leave us speechless with admiration. Let's look at them.

The Uprooting

It is winter. A bare-footed man knocks at the door of your house and asks for a pair of shoes. What do you do? Will you give him a pair? And if so, which ones, your best shoes or your worst? Your selfishness will ensure that you will give him the worst. Just try it and see.

If it's difficult for you to part with an old pair of shoes, think how difficult it would be if the Lord told you, as He did Abraham, to leave your house, your fields, and above all, your own people and go and live in a foreign country! *"Leave your country, your relatives, your father's house and come to the place I will show you,"* said God to Abraham, who was then seventy-five years old. *(Gen. 12, 1-4)*. What was his reaction?

"Come to the place I will show you," said God. He didn't go into any further details. He didn't describe to him exactly what the place was like. He didn't say: *"Where I'm telling you to go will be like Paradise"* in order to please him. And not only that—He didn't even tell him where he was going! He just left it all up in the air.

Abraham could have replied: *"God, you're telling me to go and live abroad. At least you could let me know where I'm going."* It's one thing to know where you're going and quite another to be in the dark about it. Despite this, old Abraham accepted God's command without hesitation.

Without a second thought he took his wife Sarah and his nephew Lot and set off, leaving behind his friends and relatives. Having loaded their belongings onto camels, they set off into the unknown *(Gen. 12, 5)*.

They walked and walked. Two and then three days went by. Still, God had not given him any sign of where his new home was to be. Another three days went by, even a week; but still nothing. They continued on their way, spending their nights on the roadside, traveling along paths and through rough country.

Two full weeks went by. They had covered about seven hundred and fifty kilometers. They finally reached the land of Canaan. Now, after a fortnight, God finally appeared and revealed to Abraham that this was his new homeland *(Gen. 12, 7)*.

Question 1: Why didn't God reveal his new home to him right away? Why only in the end, after keeping him in suspense for so long? He did so in order to train His good servant Abraham all the more. He did so in order to bring out the absolute confidence he had in God.

Question 2: How did Abraham manage to make such a bold decision? He laid bare his feelings and his thoughts, and he examined them. He reasoned with himself: "*God wants me to do this, but I'm reacting against it. But who thinks more clearly, God or me? So what should I do? Follow the dictates of my desires or do what God tells me?*"

Naturally, Abraham thought that his own thinking was right: *"I grew up here, this is my home. I'm doing fine here. So why should I go and live abroad. Why should I get involved in such risky business?"* And yet, he disdained, trampled upon and sacrificed his own will, submitting totally to the will of God.

Let's make a comparison. You go to confession. Your spiritual father, God's representative, tells you to do something incomparably less than what God told Abraham, and yet you resist. You insist on doing your own "God-inspired" and "wise" will. And you do it. Instead of being ashamed, you're even proud of yourself.

Remember, Abraham walked into the unknown for a fortnight. Just how inclined was the soul of Abraham to undertake this long and unheard of journey? He who had always been jolly and happy was now under stress. He was as worried as if he were going off to forced labor.

When God wants us to do something for Him, He requires that we do it with our whole hearts. It follows then, that before He gave His orders to His servant Abraham, He had already "weighed" his heart. He examined his willingness and his disposition. As the "Heart-reader" that He is, God saw that

His servant would bear this heavy cross with his whole heart. This is why He assigned it to him. To put it another way, Abraham may have been "evicted", yet he went abroad with his whole heart. Otherwise, he wouldn't have become an example to us all.

This is not to say that as a man with normal human feelings, he was not wounded in his soul. He most certainly was! How painful it must have been for him to leave his family and friends forever, with whom he had lived seventy-five whole years. But this pain was "colored" by heavenly joy and exultation. He was overshadowed by divine grace, which was granted to him as a divine gift in return for his whole-hearted and total surrender to the Lord.

The Great Sacrifice

Twenty-five years passed from the day Abraham settled in Canaan. He was now a hundred years old, while his wife Sarah was ninety *(Gen. 17, 17)*. God made it known to this elderly couple that they would have a child and that He Himself would bless this child who would become the father of many peoples *(Gen. 17, 19)*. Indeed, despite her advanced years, Sarah did have a son, Isaac.

The child grew and filled the exiled family with much joy. He reached adolescence and was a fine, upstanding boy. His father could hardly wait for the Lord to fulfill His promise when he would see his son become the father of many peoples. However, Abraham was suddenly thunderstruck! God demanded that he sacrifice his son *(Gen. 22, 1)*. What an unexpected trial! What a harsh sentence!

In Abraham's place, any ordinary mortal would surely have rebelled and cried out: *"What's all this about, God? You want me to slaughter my only son, my only hope and comfort in my exile? What have I ever done to You? Didn't You tell me that this child would become the father of many nations? So how is it that You're now telling me to sacrifice him? Did You have to choose me to crucify, after I left everything for Your sake?"* Any mortal man would have doubted God's wisdom and His love for mankind.

There was nothing of that in Abraham. He simply hastened to perform what it was that the Lord had told him to do, with complete confidence in His love for mankind. He got up early in the morning, saddled the donkey and prepared to sacrifice his son—only because that is what God commanded.

Didn't Abraham feel any pain or sorrow, as any father would, about the terrible thing he was about to do? Of course he did! Even if you kill an animal it somehow hurts. How much more if it's your one and only child! His heart was rent and torn asunder. He felt as if he was killing his own self, not his son. And yet he obeyed.

He was strengthened by the knowledge that what he was doing, he was doing at the Lord's request. It was painful, yet he did not despair. It was painful, yet he felt divine consolation.

Let's remind ourselves, Abraham left to go into exile with his whole heart. Now he was going to sacrifice his only son with his whole heart, too. He was prepared to offer his only son to God without any reservation.

This is quite clear from the following two points. First, because he was worried and troubled by the thought that at the place of sacrifice he might not find any wood, he brought some with him from his home *(Gen. 22, 3)*.

Second, Isaac was no mere child. He himself carried the wood for the sacrifice on his shoulders from the bottom of the mountain to the place where the sacrifice was to take place. He was thus already of age. Had he realized that God wanted him to be sacrificed, he would no doubt have rebelled. That's why old Abraham didn't tell him about God's decision. He wanted to prevent any such reaction. He fooled him by saying that they were going to sacrifice a ram to God.

In other words, if Abraham hadn't been prepared to sacrifice his son with all his heart, he would have done it out of a sense of duty and he would have tried to find some excuse for avoiding it. One way would have been to tell Isaac, in the hope that the latter would rebel, to reject any such idea out of hand and for Abraham to then "try to convince" him to go along, without success. Then he would have been able to say to God: *"See God, there's nothing I can do. Sorry."*

The Dramatic Journey

Isaac spent his last moments in his father's house. Old Abraham watched him. They then set off. The difficult journey lasted three days *(Gen. 22, 4)*. Every step, every word and every movement of Isaac must have been very painful for Abraham.

"Wait here with the donkey at the foot of the hill," said Abraham to his servants, *"my son and I will go up, pay our respects and then come back down" (Gen. 22, 5)*. He loaded the

wood onto Isaac. He himself took the knife and the means to light the fire and up they went.

Isaac still didn't understand what was being played out. *"Father?"* he asked. *"What is it, son?" "Where is the sheep we are going to sacrifice to the Lord?" "God will provide, my son" (Gen. 22, 7-8).*

They reached the top. With his own hands Abraham prepared the rough stone altar where the sacrifice was to take place. When he put on the wood for the burnt offering, Isaac finally realized what was happening.

Being a young man, he could easily have run off and disappeared. But he too submitted himself to the will of his Heavenly Father! He became a "self-less" person with no "self will" in the hands of Abraham, allowing his feet to be tied. Abraham then placed him on the wood and picked up the knife . . .

The Aftermath

At the critical moment, God intervened. He sent an angel from heaven to prevent Abraham from sacrificing his son. *"Abraham! Abraham!" "Yes God, I am listening." "You are not to sacrifice your son. You have proved to Me that you truly do fear Me. Because you have showed no mercy even to your beloved son, I am here to assure you that your descendants will be more numerous than the stars in the sky or the grains of sand in the sea. They will all be richly blessed" (Gen. 22, 11-17).*

The Lord now richly rewarded Abraham. And who would say that he did not deserve it? God spoke to Abraham, as He also spoke to Cain. He urged the former to sacrifice his son and the latter to repent. Cain was unmoved by God's pleas. Abraham obeyed right away.

Our Own Sacrifice

There's a story about a man who goes on a journey. As he is walking along a road, he finds a handful of nuts. Being hungry, he eats the kernels and is left with the husks. He had to do something with them, since he couldn't eat them. So what did he do? He offered them to God!

If he really wanted to make an offering to God, he should have offered the whole nuts, including the kernels. If not all of them, he should of at least offered some of them. But no, he preferred to offer only the husks.

Even if we concede that he did well to offer the husks, when did he offer them? Only at the end, after he had finished eating. What is more, he had the false impression that he had done his duty to God!

Of course our conscience condemns this action on the part of the traveler. But aren't we perhaps often like him? Don't we at times perhaps waste the substance of our lives on a thousand and one secular matters that are totally unrelated to God? Don't we too then offer only what is left over as a sacrifice to the Lord, like when we barely find time to get ourselves to church or fast as little as possible, and so on and so forth?

We should compare the "sacrifices" we make for God, keeping in mind that we live *after* Christ and even *in* Christ, with those made by Abraham who lived *before* Him. Indeed, this should give all of us reason to pause for thought . . .

CHAPTER FIVE: SODOM AND GOMORRAH

To sin is human. To persist in sin is demonic. Impenitence is thus satanic, since it is Satan who does not repent. At the time of Noah, people were punished with death not because they sinned, but because they did not repent. They had become demons instead of fulfilling their true potential as human beings. This is the reason the Lord of All utterly destroyed the inhabitants of Sodom and Gomorrah by fire! Let's look briefly at the flow of events.

The Hospitality of Abraham

It was mid-day. Abraham was sitting at the door of his tent that was pitched next to the oak of Mamre. Suddenly he saw three strangers approaching. He ran to meet them. Bowing down, he begged to offer them hospitality. They consented.

He fetched water to cool them and told his wife Sarah to prepare food. He himself ran off to the herd to select the best animal to slaughter. He gave it to his servants and ordered them to set the table. The three strangers were two angels and the Lord Almighty. Having enjoyed the hospitality of Abraham, they set off for Sodom and Gomorrah. Abraham accompanied them.

God "adores" His genuine servants, to such an extent that He doesn't hesitate to reveal His secrets to them. At an earlier time, He had confided to Noah that He was going to destroy the world *(Gen. 6, 13)*. Now He did the same with Abraham. As they were going along, He explained to the two angels: *"I have no intention of hiding what I am about to do from my servant Abraham. I hear many loud cries from Sodom and Gomorrah. They are committing great sins. I want to see if things really are as bad as I hear. I want to know."*[7] The two angels continued on their way to Sodom. The Lord stayed outside the town, with Abraham standing beside him.

Six Times (!)

The tender-hearted Abraham was extremely sad when he heard from the Lord that the town was to be destroyed. He went up to Him and pleaded with Him on behalf of the town. He started a long and lively discussion with the Lord, speaking to Him in a bold and

---

[7] Of course, as God, Who knows all things, He already knew what was going on in Sodom. But He wanted to make an "on the spot inspection" to teach us not to be gullible and believe whatever comes to our ears.

familiar way as if He were a friend. Not only that, but every so often he set new terms. The Good Lord was always positive towards Abraham. But when He saw that His beloved servant had stopped negotiating, He proceeded with the destruction.

It is truly amazing! Abraham put the following six different proposals before the Lord during the discussion. The Lord agreed to them all without the slightest objection.

First: Abraham said to God: *"If there's fifty righteous people in the town, surely they won't be destroyed along with the unrighteous? Won't You save the town for their sake? You would never do anything like that!"* God replied: *"If there are fifty righteous people in the town, it will be saved for their sake."*

Second: Now Abraham knew that it would be extremely difficult, if not impossible, to find fifty righteous people, so he "renegotiated". *"Suppose there's not fifty, but only forty-five people, surely you won't destroy the town because there are only five righteous people short?" "No, I will not destroy it,"* replied the Lord.

Third: It would have been difficult enough to find even that many righteous people in Sodom, so Abraham came down even further.

"If there are only forty?" "Again, for their sake, the town will not be destroyed."

Fourth: It seems that Abraham was beginning to feel uncomfortable about "twisting God's arm". Yet at the same time, he didn't want Sodom to be destroyed. Seeing the goodness of God, he felt compelled to continue his struggle. He politely and rather cunningly asks God, *"Lord, will it annoy You if I speak again?"* Then, without waiting for an answer, he came back to the same old thing: *"Suppose there are only thirty righteous?"* Far from being annoyed, the Lord answered positively: *"For their sake, the town will not be destroyed."*

Fifth: Seeing that God kept giving way to him, Abraham went even further: *"Twenty?"* Again, the Lord affirmed, *"The town will be saved!"* It truly is remarkable. The more "persistent" the servant became, the more lenient was the Lord.

Sixth: Abraham began thinking again. He didn't think it at all polite on his part to be bargaining with the Lord. But he couldn't rest on account of his compassion for Sodom. He went on, employing the same mixture of politeness and cunning: *"Lord, are You sure it won't upset You if I speak just one more time?"* Again, without waiting for an answer, he asked: *"What if, in the end, there is only ten?" "Then again the town will be saved!"*

Now note this. He started with fifty and came down to ten. Abraham came down? So did God. God followed Abraham, not vice versa. He pleaded with God six times and six times the Lord consented. That's how accommodating God is with His saints.

Seeing how the Lord Almighty was giving way each time to his requests, Abraham was overwhelmed by His long-suffering goodness. He decided: *"Better that Sodom is lost than that I should "annoy" my God any longer."*

So he stopped at ten. He did not go down to five. God then left for the heavens. His servant Abraham returned to his tent a shattered man. Sodom would soon be consumed in flames.

How Lot Was Saved

The Lord knows how to save the godly from temptation *(2 Peter 2, 9)*. We have seen this with Noah. Now we will see it with Lot.

Lot was Abraham's nephew. He lived with his family in Sodom. Despite the fact that he lived in such a degenerate world, he himself was untouched by the arrows of sin. God had ensured that Noah would be saved from the

Flood. Now he saw to it that Lot would be saved from the fire. Noah was saved by the Ark; Lot was saved by two "strangers" (that is, angels), sent by the Lord.

The two strangers were none other than those who, shortly before, had enjoyed the hospitality of Abraham and had then left for Sodom. Now, towards dusk, they arrived at the town.

At the entrance sat Lot. No sooner did he see them that (in imitation of his uncle, Abraham) he ran to meet them. He bowed to them and said: *"Gentlemen, come and spend the night at my house." "No,"* they replied, *"we will stay in the square."* Lot, who had a good heart, insisted. The "strangers" relented. He had the table laid for them. They ate and were ready for sleep.

News had spread throughout the town that two men were staying at Lot's house. Everyone, both old men and young boys, all surrounded the house and started shouting out, *"Where are those two who have come to visit you at dusk? Bring them out so we can have them!"*

Lot went out, first locking the door to his house so that the angels were safe inside. *"Brethren,"* he exclaimed to the mob, *"these men are guests under my roof. They are under my protection. Please do not do them any harm!"*

Even though he spoke well to them and addressed them so politely, calling them "brethren", they became increasingly violent. *"You are a foreigner. Get out of here! Who are you to judge us? We'll rough you up even more than them."*

They surged towards him and began beating him. The angels grabbed him and pulled him inside, locking the door again. It was certain that the mob, in pursuit of their desires, would have broken down the door and killed Lot. At this critical moment, God intervened and blinded the mob.

The angels said to Lot: *"If you've got any sons or daughters in this town, any in-laws and anybody else dear to you, get them out of here."* It would seem that Lot didn't really believe them, but so as not to put them out, he went and spoke to his relations. He told them the news without mincing his words: *"Get up. Get out of the town. The Lord is going to destroy it."* Of course, they thought he was joking.

Lot returned home. It was still night. Near dawn, the two angels started pressuring him, *"Get up. Take your wife and your two daughters and get out of town."* Lot and his family did not know what to do. They now realized how critical the situation was. The angels took Lot, his wife and his daughters by the arms and led them out of the town.

"Get out of here! Save your lives. Don't look back and don't stop at the edge of the town. Go right away toward the mountain. Only in this way will you escape the catastrophe." "Lord," said Lot to the first angel, *"I will never manage to get as far as that mountain. Let me go as far as that little town there, Zoar, to be saved." "I will do you that favor. For your sake, that town will not be destroyed. Hurry there now. I will not act until you get there."*[8]

Although the angel had given strict instructions to them not to look back, Lot's wife couldn't help herself. She was undone by her curiosity. She deliberately disregarded the command of the angel and looked back. She became a pillar of salt *(Gen. 19, 26)*. The ultimate outcome of her disobedience was death.

---

[8] The angels could have helped Lot and his family to get to that town, too. But they didn't. The family could now do so by themselves. Thus we see how angels (and God) intervene and help us when we can't be helped by ourselves or our fellows.

The Terrible Destruction

"The sun had risen upon the earth when Lot entered Zoar. Then, from out of the heavens, God rained fire and brimstone upon Sodom and Gomorrah" (Gen. 19, 23-24).

The sun was up, Lot was now out of danger and at once the catastrophe began. It rained fire and brimstone! The whole place caught fire! What a terrible sight!

Early in the morning Abraham went to the site where the day before, shortly after noon, he had pleaded with the Lord to save Sodom. He looked towards the town and the surrounding villages and saw fire rising up out of the earth *(Gen. 19, 28)*. The place was a furnace, with people being roasted alive. What appalling scenes! What screams! What cries! Everyone and everything was "carbonized" forever.

All that's left of the Flood are the remains of the Ark that science has uncovered and which survive to this day. All that's left of Sodom and Gomorrah is the destruction itself. To this day, they remain uninhabited. They resemble a cemetery. Moreover, no animal—wild or tame—will live there. The Dead Sea is quite literally "dead". Not a thing lives there. Even birds avoid flying over it because they are choked by the sulfuric fumes and so they change direction. Could this be an eternal sign of Divine Justice? *(cf. 2 Peter 2, 6).*

God is Judge

Do you see how, although He loves mankind, the Lord will punish, and indeed even unto death? This is because God is not only the Lover of Mankind, but also the Universal Judge. Perhaps at times it is more beneficial for our souls to see God as the Incorruptible Judge, rather than only as the Lover of Mankind *(cf. Saint John Climacus, The Ladder of Divine Ascent, 6, 11).*

Saint John Chrysostom brings this example of the destruction of Sodom and Gomorrah to any "lover of the flesh" who doesn't believe that the All-merciful God is, at the same time, a chastiser. He writes: *"Because you don't see Hell* (that is, punishment) *now before your eyes, you deny it. But can you not believe something that happened in the past? Just think for a minute about Sodom and Gomorrah. No other land was punished as severely as they were. And they were punished because the inhabitants were "lovers of the flesh". How is it possible for God, Who is always the same, to punish the Sodomites for their sins and not punish you, who live after Christ and have received so much grace and yet continue to live in sin? Indeed, you will be punished much worse than Sodom and Gomorrah (Homily on the Israelites under the Cloud).*

Chapter Six: Joseph (Part 1)

Abraham was the father of Isaac; Isaac was the father of Jacob; Jacob was the father of Joseph. Joseph was therefore the grandson of Isaac and the great-grandson of Abraham. His father Jacob had twelve sons, including Benjamin and Joseph who were born in his old age by his wife Rachel. In other words, Joseph and Benjamin were full brothers, born of the same mother. The story of Joseph is both very instructive and at the same time very exciting. Let's look at it carefully.

The First Blow: Envy

Old Jacob was particularly fond of Joseph and he showed it in a number of ways. He even had a beautiful coat of many colors made for him. But this fondness annoyed the other brothers. They envied and hated their brother, just as Cain had done before them.

One morning, Joseph told his brothers about some strange dreams he'd had: "*You were binding sheaves in the middle of the field. My sheaf was standing straight while all yours were bowing down to it.*" "*Does this mean that you will become king and lord over us?*" Their hatred increased even more.

Joseph had another dream that he told to the whole family: "*It seemed to me that the sun and moon were bowing to me, together with eleven stars.*" "*What sort of a dream is that,*" asked his father, berating him, "*do you think that I, your mother and your brothers are going to come and bow down to you?*" His brothers envied him all the more.

His brothers left the house. They went to the region of Shechem, where they grazed their sheep. There they stayed. Shechem was about ninety kilometers from Hebron, about three days on foot. Jacob said to Joseph: "*Go to Shechem and see how your brothers and the sheep are doing. Then come back and tell me.*" Joseph did as he was told.

When his brothers saw him from afar they wanted (in imitation of Cain) to murder him. "*Look,*" they said among themselves, "*here comes the dreamer of dreams* (they hadn't forgotten). *Let's kill him and throw him into a pit. Then we'll see the value of his dreams.*"

Reuben, who was the eldest, tried to intervene: "*Let us not do such a thing. It is better to put him down a dry well. At least do not kill him.*" It was Reuben's intention to raise him up out of the well and return him to his father. The brothers gave in. They laid hands on Joseph. They took his coat of many colors.

Then they all dragged him angrily and threw him down the well. Joseph started crying. He begged them, *"Don't do this to me."* They were unmoved, however, and down he went.

Young Joseph was now lying in the well. He was consumed by the dark and the loneliness. At the same time, there was a question in his pure soul: *"Why have my brothers done this to me? Why?"* Above ground, the troublemakers were beginning to feel very uneasy.

At that very moment a caravan of Ishmaelite merchants was passing on its way to Egypt. "*What do we gain by killing our brother?*" asked Judas. "*Why don't we sell him to the Ishmaelites? He's our brother, after all. Our own flesh and blood.*" So they got rid of him by selling him off.

The passion of envy convinced them to kill him. Conscience told them, *"No, he's our brother."* A civil war was taking place within them. They were trying to disarm their conscience. But of course, they could not. In the end, they found the answer—compromise! In this way, they satisfied their passion and they also "satisfied" (that is they "fooled") their conscience, just as a thief does when he steals or an adulterer does committing adultery, etc.

Although Reuben was away, when he came back he went straight to the well to see Joseph. When he saw the well empty, he rent his clothes because of his great sorrow. He met his brothers and with great sadness told them: *"Joseph's gone! I am the eldest, and thus I am responsible. Now what do I do?"*

The real problem was what they were going to tell their father Jacob. His cunning sons found the solution—they would try to fool him. They smeared Joseph's beautiful coat with goat's blood and went to their father and told him: *"We found this. Have a look and see if it belongs to Joseph."*

"This is Joseph's coat. It's my son's. A wild animal must have devoured him." Jacob rent his clothes. He put on special black sackcloth and mourned forty days. His relatives tried to comfort him, as did his sons. The wretched brothers thought that by what they'd done, they'd buried Joseph's future for him. How were they to know that, in fact, they had set him up for life?

The Second Blow: Slander

Seventeen-year-old Joseph arrived in Egypt. On one hand, he had escaped the clutches of his envious brothers, but on the other he was lost in the unknown. He had no idea what was awaiting him.

The Ishmaelite merchant who had bought him didn't keep him for his own purposes. He sold him to Potiphar, the chief cook of the Pharaoh. Potiphar held Joseph in great esteem and allowed him a free hand in the running of his household. But here he found a new trial.

"And Joseph was handsome in form and exceedingly beautiful in countenance" (Gen. 39, 6). The wife of Potiphar conceived a sexual desire for him. They were together every day at the house and she tempted him in many ways and on many occasions. But Joseph remained steadfast.

The wicked woman could not resist the temptation. She pulled him by his garment, a kind of tunic that they wore, and said: *"Come and lay down with me in bed."* Apparently she pulled him with such force that the tunic slipped off his body and she was left with it in her hands.

Joseph was standing there with no clothes on and there was this woman next to him trying to seduce him. Yet even at this critical moment it did not occur to him to give in to the temptation and to sin. He literally ran away from the temptation, running away from her and out onto the street, naked as he was, crushing down the desires of the flesh.

"Hell hath no fury like a woman scorned." The seductress called her household servants: "*You see. My husband brings a Hebrew slave into the house and he tries to get me to sleep with him. But I started shouting right away. And now he has disappeared, leaving his clothes behind.*" She told her husband the same thing and he became very angry *(Gen. 39, 19)*. The wife had "material evidence". The "guilty party" was caught and thrown into prison.

God Stands By Us

So far, the pure-hearted Joseph had certainly suffered the slings and arrows of an outrageous fortune. He'd been thrown down a dry well like a piece of rubbish. He'd been sold as a slave. He had been jailed as a criminal. Yet, not long before, he'd seen some exceptional dreams that suggested that one day everyone would be bowing down before him. Still, for the present, there was "no light at the end of the tunnel"—no light at all!

It is true that at these difficult times, Joseph was bereft of any human support. But he had the support of our Merciful and Loving God: *"And God was with him,"* as we are told in Holy Scripture *(Acts 7, 9)*. God was indeed with Joseph, because Joseph was with God. He demonstrated that in practice. For His sake, he did not sin with the wife of Potiphar: *"How shall I do this wicked thing and sin against God" (Gen. 39, 9)*.

This very thought was enough for him to tame that wild beast, that is, the "flesh". Just think what awe the holy name of God must have occasioned in his soul. In his soul, however, he was still bowed down with the burden of injustice and contempt.

But God, Who *"raises the poor out of the dust, and lifts the needy out of the ash heap" (Psalm 113, 7)* did not leave His faithful servant in such a destitute state. He raised him up, to such an extent that all his tribulations turned out for the good, in accordance with the words of Saint Paul: *"To those who love God, everything works to the good" (Rom. 8, 28)*.

Let's examine the admirable plan that God laid out in order to bring Joseph out of dishonor and contempt, and to raise him up in terms of honor and glory. From the shame as an insignificant slave, the Lord raised him up high, to the position of a glorious king!

Into the same prison where Joseph was cast were also thrown two of Pharaoh's officials.

One was the chief cup-bearer and the other the chief baker. God made use of this predicament, as He can do in each and every predicament in which we may find ourselves. These officials had some strange dreams and they were greatly worried. They told Joseph about them. God used this as well. He enlightened Joseph so that he was able to interpret the dreams.

"In three days, they will hang you," he told the chief baker, as indeed, they did. *"In three days you will be back at the palace in your old position,"* he told the chief cup-bearer, *"and please, when you're free, go to Pharaoh and get him to do something about me. I am unjustly being held here in prison."* In three days the chief cup-bearer was indeed returned to his post.

Two years went by and Joseph was still in prison. The chief cup-bearer had forgotten all about him. Isn't that the way it is! How easily people forget! People may forget, but not God! God now saw to it that Joseph came out of prison and, moreover, with much glory and honor. This is how it happened . . .

Pharaoh also had some strange nightmares. He saw in a dream that he was standing beside the Nile River. Out of the river came seven fat cows, which grazed on the banks of the

Nile. After them, seven lean cows came up out of the river and they ate the fat ones. Strange! A very unusual dream indeed! How was it that seven lean cows should eat seven fat ones?

Pharaoh awoke in terror, but he went back to sleep. He had the same dream again, and again he awoke in terror. After that, he could not fall back to sleep. Day broke. It was impossible for Pharaoh to calm down. He was too upset by the dreams. He sent for all the interpreters of dreams and the wise men of Egypt, but no one could explain to him how the seven lean cattle had eaten the seven fat ones. The chief cup-bearer finally spoke to Pharaoh about Joseph's abilities of interpreting dreams. Pharaoh at once had a man sent to the prison to bring Joseph to the palace.

This was a great honor for the despised Joseph. The moment arrived for him to be presented to Pharaoh. The suspense was unbearable. What explanation would he give to these enigmatic dreams?

God, Who was controlling the whole of this story behind the scenes, again appeared on stage. He enlightened Joseph's intellect so that he was able to interpret the dreams: *"The seven fat cows,"* he said, *"mean that seven years will come when the fruits of the earth will be plentiful. The seven lean cows, on the other hand, mean that afterwards there will be seven years of famine, which will destroy the country."* He advised Pharaoh to see to it that during the seven years of plenty, food was stored for the difficult years that would follow.

Pharaoh was delighted. He appointed Joseph his Regent over Egypt! Joseph was then thirty years old. God acted to ensure that Joseph's successive trials were all crowned with brilliant success.[9] He who was most unjustly treated, was in the end restored and showered with glory by God Himself.

There now begins another adventure that is even more dramatic—the adventure with his brothers.

---

[9] There are two things worthy of note here. First, when God wanted to bring glory to Joseph, He didn't send angels from heaven to carry out His plan. He used people, who were, moreover, idolaters: Pharaoh and his chief cup-bearer. Second, while His plan was being carried out, God worked in the background without fuss, silently and secretly. That is how He works in our lives, too—through people, and more often than not, silently and secretly.

CHAPTER SEVEN: JOSEPH (Part 2)

It's a small world, as they say. And indeed, how many times do we meet people with whom we have lost touch, and what's more, where we'd least expect to do so? Something similar now happened with Joseph's brothers.

Twenty years before, they had sold him as a slave. Since then, they had lost all trace of him. They had no idea whether he was dead or alive. Even if it ever occurred to them that they might come across him some day, they would never have imagined that it would be as Regent of Egypt!

They Seek Food

The seven years of plenty arrived. Joseph filled all the warehouses of Egypt with corn, *"like the sand of the sea" (Gen. 41, 49)*. Then came the seven lean years. The earth stopped producing. Both Egypt and Canaan (Joseph's homeland) and all their cities and peoples were beset by the scourge of famine.

Caravans from all over arrived in Egypt to buy corn. *"Any time now,"* thought Joseph, *"my family will come. Including my own beloved brother, Benjamin."*

Twenty years had passed since he'd been "separated" from them. He was then seventeen years old; now he was thirty-seven. Being a good soul, he longed to see them, especially Benjamin. In order not to miss them, he commanded that any people who came from Canaan were to be sent directly to his own office.

"What are you sitting around here for," Jacob said to his sons, *"I've heard there's corn for sale in Egypt. Go and buy some, so that we don't die from hunger."* He did not send Benjamin with them, however, out of fear that something might happen to him on the way.

The ten brothers had arrived in Egypt. They came as far as the palace. As Canaanites, they were taken directly to the Regent. Naturally, they all bowed down before him.

Joseph recognized them at a glance. He also remembered the dreams he had twenty years before, which had aroused their envy. He now had standing before him those who had plotted his death and who had wounded him at such a tender age when, more than anything, he needed their protection.

He struggled with himself. Should he tell them who he was or not? His emotions were compelling him to do so. These were critical moments indeed. As a human being, he could express his grievance and hurt his brothers, who had come from so far away. But there was also the danger that he would allow his passions to run riot and take his revenge. Being as disciplined as he was, he conquered his passions and feelings.

Benjamin, his beloved full brother, was the only one who was not there. This started Joseph thinking. He was worried. What could have happened? Had his brothers killed him? Or perhaps they were envious of him too, and wanted to make him suffer.

In order to get to the bottom of things, he proceeded to set two tests. By the first, he'd find out if Benjamin were alive or not. By the second, he'd learn if they were envious of him or not. In order for the tests to succeed, he deemed it better not to reveal his identity to them. In order to remove any suspicion from their minds, he spoke to them through an interpreter.

First Test: Is Benjamin Alive?

Joseph could hardly ask his brothers directly *"How is my brother Benjamin?"* That would have given away his plan. So he began by asking some completely unrelated questions that gradually and naturally brought the subject around to Benjamin.

"Where are you from?" "We've come from Canaan to buy corn." "No! You've come to spy on my land. You are spies!" "No, Lord. We are peaceable men. Your servants are not spies." "No, you have come to spy out the weaknesses of my country." "We are twelve brothers who live in Canaan. The youngest is living there with our father, the other one is gone for good." "I have told you that you are spies. If indeed you are telling the truth, it will come out. Bring me your youngest brother. Otherwise, you can not leave." He sent them off to prison for three days.

On the third day, he summoned them and told them again: *"If you are not spies, do as I tell you. One of you will stay here in prison. The rest of you will take corn back to your father. And if you do not bring your youngest brother to me, your brother will be killed."*

Their consciences were now bothering them. *"We are in this mess,"* they said among themselves, *"because we were in the wrong in regard to our brother Joseph."* Reuben said, *"I told you at the time not to harm the child. But did you listen to me? Well, we are paying for it now."*

They were talking in their native tongue, with the impression that the Regent could not understand them. Joseph could understand them, however, and he broke down crying. So as not to give himself away, he drew aside and burst into tears. Then he went back to them. He spoke to them again and told them that he would keep Symeon as a hostage. At the same time, he told his servants to fill all their sacks with corn, to return the money they had paid and to provide them with food for the journey.

They arrived back in Canaan. They had to tell their father Jacob about their unexpected trial. When they told him that Benjamin had to present himself in Egypt, it was as if an arrow had struck Jacob's heart.

"You have left me without children. My beloved Joseph is gone forever. Now Symeon is not here as well. Do you really expect to take Benjamin away from me, too? It is just one evil after another." "If you give me Benjamin," said Reuben, *"I swear I will bring him back. And if I do not, may my own two sons die." "No,"* answered their father, *"he is all that is left to me from my wife Rachel. I fear that something will happen to him and I will go down to the nether world with bitter poison in my soul."*

Misery from the famine became even more intense in Canaan. The corn they'd brought back from Egypt was coming to an end. *"Go back to Egypt and buy more corn,"* said Jacob to his sons. *"But Father,"* said Judas, *"we told you the Regent warned us clearly not to come back without our youngest brother. Please give us Benjamin and we will go. If you refuse, we can not go."*

"You went and told him you had another brother! Do you know what evil you've done to me?" "He insisted himself on learning about our family. He asked us if our father was still alive and if we had another brother. How were we to know he'd want us to bring him to him?"

Judas pleaded with his father, *"Please send Benjamin with me and we will set off now. I will take full responsibility for him. You will get him back from my own hands; we are just wasting our time with all this talking. We could have been to Egypt and back twice by now!" "Well,"* said Jacob in the end, *"if that's the way things are, do as you think best."*

So off they went with Benjamin, with twice the money for corn and with many gifts for the harsh Regent, in hope of making him more amenable. When they finally arrived in Egypt, they went directly to the Regent. Joseph finally saw his brother Benjamin. He glanced at him quickly and then returned to his everyday tasks. The private and critical meeting was fixed for later that day.

The moment came. His brothers came to his private residence, bearing gifts. They dropped to the floor and prostrated themselves. *"How are you,"* asked Joseph, *"and how is your old father you were telling me about? Is he still alive?" "Your servant our father is well,"* they replied. *"Your father is truly blessed by God,"* said Joseph, fixing his gaze on Benjamin again. *"Is this the brother that you said you'd bring with you? God be merciful to you, my son."* His spirit was in turmoil. So as not to show it, he went into his own room and began to weep. After he'd washed his face, he returned to them.

"Prepare the table," he said to his servants. At the meal, Benjamin was given the best portion. Joseph gave orders that the "strangers" were to sit at the table according to their age. On the right, next to Joseph sat the eldest, then the next oldest and so on. His brothers were rather surprised at being asked to sit in order of age.

Second Test: Do They Envy Benjamin?

Joseph devised the following plan to learn whether or not the brothers envied Benjamin. Benjamin would be arrested as a "thief" and Joseph would then hold him hostage. If his brothers were envious of him and wanted to do him ill, they would not react. On the contrary, they would be happy and go on their way in peace. If they really loved him, however, they would do anything possible to get him released. Let's see what happened.

Joseph gave orders to his servants to fill sacks with corn. They were also ordered to put a silver cup in Benjamin's sack, without him knowing it. Day dawned. The "strangers" were given permission to return home. Off they set, full of pride and joy. No sooner did they reach the outskirts of the town, however, than a black cloud descended on their hearts.

A messenger from Joseph ran up, panting: "*Why have you been so ungrateful,*" he asked, "*why have you stolen my lord's silver cup?*" The brothers were confused and terrified.

"*God forbid,*" they cried out, "*we would not do a thing like that. Search us. You can kill whomever has the cup. The rest of us will become servants to your master.*" The messenger agreed.

The brothers quickly unloaded their sacks. The messenger searched through them all, beginning with the sack that belonged to the eldest, Reuben. He finally found the cup—in Benjamin's sack!

What a sickening blow that was for them! In their great distress, the brothers cried out and ripped apart their clothes. They loaded up the sacks and returned to the town. They had to account for themselves.

It was still morning and Joseph had not yet left his house. They presented themselves before him, Judas in front, and the rest behind him. They fell down and prostrated before him. It was time for the interrogation. "*Why did you do this thing?*" "*What can we say,*" answered Judas, "*what excuse can we give? God has found some sin and has punished us for it. See! We are all your servants now.*" "*No, not all of you will become my servants. I want only the one in whose sack the cup was found. The rest of you may return to your father.*" Judas went up to Joseph and pleaded, "*Please,*" he said, "*allow me to speak to you.*"

He tried to persuade him that if old Jacob did not see Benjamin, he would die of heartbreak. "*Instead of Benjamin,*" continued Judas, "*let me remain as your servant. Let Benjamin return with my brothers to our aged father. There is no way I can go home without Benjamin. I could not bear to witness the distress it would cause my father.*"

Joseph was watching the whole drama unfold with concealed joy. He now realized that his brothers were not envious of Benjamin. On the contrary, they obviously loved him. They were even prepared to sacrifice themselves for him.

The Crowning Moment

His love for his brothers now increased even further. His pure heart was overflowing and ready to burst. The moment had come to reveal himself to them. He could not contain himself. He shouted out so loud that he could be heard outside: *"It is me, your brother Joseph! Is my father still alive? Come here close to me. It is me, Joseph, the brother that you sold into slavery!"*

What an amazing scene, with such mixed emotions of both joy and shame. How should they react to such emotions? Should they run and embrace him? But how to embrace him, after they'd thrown him down a well and sold him, as if he had been their slave?

It was their wounded and wronged brother himself who provided them with a way out —and so tenderly, too. Not a word of blame or reproach passed his lips! *"Don't be sad,"* he told them, *"it was God who brought me here,* ***before*** *you and* ***for*** *you. We are now in the* *second lean year. Another five are on the way. It was not you who sent me, but God. Now, go back to my father. Tell him to come and live here with me. We can all live here together!"*

Weeping and with much emotion, Joseph hugged and kissed Benjamin, doing the same with the rest of his brothers as well.

CHAPTER EIGHT: JOSEPH (Part 3)

The hearts of Joseph's brothers were troubled. Twenty years earlier, they were willing to hurt their father Jacob by telling him that Joseph was no longer alive and that he had been devoured by wild beasts. Now they had to tell him that Joseph was not only alive, but that indeed he was doing very well. But how?

This could have caused a great rift between them. One might have said to the other: *"It's all your fault that we made a fool of our father."* They might even have come to blows. Finally, for the common good, they found the answer. They remembered that they had announced Joseph's "death" to their father all together *(Gen. 37, 32)*. Now, they would also announce the joyful tidings all together as well *(Gen. 45, 26)*.

Joseph did not know about the trick they had played on their father. He was under the impression that they told him the truth. *"Do not become troubled along the way,"* he advised them *(Gen. 45, 24)*, that is, *"Don't blame each other for selling me off. Let bygones be bygones."* He gave them many valuable gifts, as well as chariots with which to transport their father and their families. They set off.

From Canaan to Egypt

Back in Canaan, Jacob was all alone. He was consumed with anxiety: "*What on earth is going on in Egypt? What has happened to my son, Benjamin? Has he been kept as a hostage, like Symeon? Or perhaps he's been eaten by animals, like Joseph!*" He longed to hear news and waited anxiously for it.

And then, suddenly, there were his sons arriving (at long last) from Egypt. He saw the laden pack animals. That was a good sign. Then . . . he saw Benjamin! Hardly had he recovered when a real bombshell fell on his ears.

Without any further ado, his sons told him: *"Your son, Joseph, is alive. He is Regent in Egypt—and what is more—he is waiting for us!" "Jacob was amazed" (Gen. 45, 26).* He couldn't understand what they were telling him. He couldn't believe their words. But when he saw the chariots that had come to take him, he believed and said: *"It is a great thing for me that my son, Joseph, is alive. I shall go and see him before I die."*

His grandfather Abraham had settled in Canaan (i.e., the Promised Land) on the instructions of God. Jacob was now faced with a problem of *conscience.* Could he leave the

Promised Land and go to Egypt? Wouldn't that be showing contempt for God?

His paternal instinct was bringing unbearable pressure on him to go and see his son, but his conscience rebelled! He turned to the Good Lord to show him if it was His will that he should go to Egypt. If not, he would not go. He was willing to die without seeing his son! He went to the *"well of the oath"* and offered a sacrifice to God, and he waited.

The Lord, seeing his genuine intentions, appeared to him in a vision: *"Jacob, Jacob!" "What is it, Lord?" "It is I, the God of your fathers. Do not be afraid to go down to Egypt."* In order to encourage him, He promised him: *"There I shall make a great nation of you. I shall go down with you. At the right time, I will bring you back to Canaan. Joseph will close your eyes."*[10]

---

[10] How generously God answers! He didn't simply give him "permission", but assured him that He would even accompany him and also that He would make him glorious! He also told him that at the end of his life it would be Joseph who would "close his eyes" (that is, bury him) as he had so much hoped for. God is so good and generous to all those who open their hearts to Him. How hard-hearted we are, when we close our souls to Him and do not let Him show His mercy and goodness to us.

A Moment to Savor

With God's blessing, Jacob set off for Egypt. As they entered Egypt, in the region of Goshen, Jacob sent Judas on ahead as a "herald". The time came for him to see his beloved son, whom he had given up for dead.

Joseph harnessed his royal chariot and sped off. They hadn't seen each other for twenty years. And now, they met! Joseph, as the younger man, was first to run to his father and embrace him: *"He fell upon his neck and wept great tears" (Gen. 46, 29).* Jacob exclaimed, *"Now I do not mind if I die; for I have seen you once again, and you are still alive."*

Joseph then settled his brothers *"on the best land" (Gen. 47, 11),* i. e., on the most fertile land in Egypt. As long as the famine lasted, he cared for them personally, so that his brothers and their families were sure of their portion *(Gen. 47, 12).* What a forgiving attitude!

Jacob's Swan Song

Seventeen years passed from the day Jacob came to settle in the land of Egypt. He was now one hundred and forty-seven years old, a ripe old age. He already felt the onset of the end of his days. *"Place of birth, place of rest,"* says a Greek proverb. Jacob felt the same. He summoned Joseph and told him his last wish: *"Please, do me this favor: swear that when I die you will not bury me in Egypt, but in Canaan, with my parents."* Having sworn to do so, Joseph returned to his duties in the palace.

Jacob took to his bed. His condition worsened. They notified Joseph. The dying man tried to sit up in bed. He summoned his other children. They saw him for the last time, the father to whom they brought so much bitterness. Gathered around him, they received his blessing, one by one. They heard his last instructions and received his final blessing.

This dying father, who was well over a hundred years old, still found the strength to speak separately with each one his twelve sons. He spoke to them for so long and so peacefully that one might have thought that he wasn't about to die at all. Yet there he was, on the threshold of death!

When he had finished he said: *"I am dying. Bury me in the cave next to the oak of Mamre, where Abraham buried his wife Sarah; where they buried Isaac and his wife Rebecca, and where I, too, buried my wife Leah.* His speech was cut short. He raised his feet and lay down on the bed, and he died in peace.

Joseph fell upon the face of his dead father and covered him with kisses and tears. The funeral was to take place in his homeland, in accordance with his deepest wishes. The procession set off.

The great man was accompanied by his sons, his daughters-in-law, his grandchildren and all his relatives. As a mark of honor to Joseph, the Regent of Egypt, all of Pharaoh's servants accompanied the procession, as did the elders of the palace and the provincial governors.

Near the River Jordan, at the threshing-floor of Atad, they stopped. The mourners bitterly lamented the passing of Jacob. The mourning for him lasted seven days. When the inhabitants of Canaan saw the long funeral procession and heard the loud lamentations that issued from the threshing-floor of Atad, they said: *"There is great mourning in Egypt."* Henceforth, the place was known as "The Mourning of Egypt".

Jacob was buried in his homeland in the tomb of his fathers. His many children, his grandchildren, his relations and all those accompanying them returned to Egypt.[11]

Guilty Consciences

His brothers now began to worry. *"Now that our father is dead,"* they thought, *"maybe Joseph will find an opportunity to get his revenge for what we did to him."* They reasoned that they had better do something to head off any impending trouble.

They had seen how Joseph was extremely fond of his father, and so they tried to exploit this. They went and told him: *"Before your father died, he bound us on oath, saying to us: 'Tell Joseph to forgive the wrong you did him'. So forgive the injustice committed by the servants of God and of your father. You see, we are all your servants."*[12] Joseph would

---

[11] Jacob's "family" remained four hundred and thirty years in Egypt *(Ex. 12, 40)*. They grew and multiplied until they were the dominant population. It was then that another Pharaoh decided to get rid of the "foreign" Hebrews. Moses belonged to the descendants of the brothers of Joseph. Once he'd reached the age of forty, God called on him to liberate his compatriots and lead them back into the Promised Land.

[12] Interestingly, what they withheld from their father, because it was then to their advantage, they now used as their "way out". Such is the thought process of self-interest, and indeed of every passion.

surely have wondered: *"Why didn't my father tell me this himself?"* No doubt he smelled a rat. But now, too, he showed the nobility of his spirit. He listened to them and wept with emotion.

"Do not worry," he told them, *"I am a man of God. You thought to deal wickedly with me, but God thought to deal well with me, so that what came about might be possible and that so many people could be fed. Do not worry. I will feed you."* He continued to talk to them. He spoke in such a way that he calmed their souls. It wasn't his passions that spoke—it was his love. Love always accepts and always shows patience. Love never fails.

The Death of Joseph

Life is so short. It seems as if we "gallop" towards death. At age seventeen, Joseph was sold as a slave. For thirteen years he was an object of contempt; yet for a total of eighty years, he was Regent. How glorious God had made him! Once a youth of seventeen, he was now a hundred and ten years old. The years had simply flown by.

Like his father before him, he too felt his end approaching. Like his father before him, he too was untroubled and peaceful at the thought of his passing away. On his death-bed, he said to his family: *"I am dying now, but God will visit you and bring you back to the land of your fathers. When you go back home, take my bones with you."* Then he gave up his spirit peacefully, as do the servants of the Lord.

His Teacher

Joseph lived before Christ. He had no examples of forbearance to follow. Not only that, when he was alive, not even the Ten Commandments had yet been handed down! Who taught him to behave with such forbearance towards his brothers? It was his conscience!

Joseph acted in accordance with his conscience. Wherever he was, he always paid attention to its slightest movement. The more he paid attention to it, the more refined and cleansed his conscience became. Cain too, who killed Abel, had a conscience, but he did not listen to its voice. Look where he ended up.

Do *we* always and everywhere proceed according to our conscience, or do we at times trample it underfoot?

Chapter Nine: Job

On Top of the World

Job wasn't just anybody. He had many good features that elevated him in the eyes of society. He had ten children and he was enormously wealthy, with five hundred she-asses, one thousand oxen, three thousand camels and seven thousand sheep, as well as boundless lands and countless servants. He lived a righteous life and was very charitable. As Job himself said, *"I was eyes to the blind, and feet to the lame. I was a father to the poor" (Job 29, 15-16).*

His enormous wealth and great virtue gave him status. Everyone respected him. He was well-known, his fame even reached beyond the borders of his own land to the boundaries of the known world. He was known to kings and princes, indeed to everyone.

When he went to town in the morning and walked along the streets, the young people didn't dare look him in the face. The elders stood up out of respect. The community leaders would stop talking and put their fingers to their lips, showing the others to be quiet too *(Job 29, 7-10).*

Into Chaos

One day, his ten children were at a social gathering at the house of the eldest. Job remained at home. While the sons and daughters of Job were enjoying themselves, a servant ran in to see him. *"Lord,"* he said, *"robbers came and they slaughtered the five-hundred she-asses! They killed the one-thousand oxen. They slew the herdsmen as well!"* What turmoil and great anxiety for Job!

He had hardly recovered when a second messenger arrived with even worse news: *"Horsemen divided into three companies and surrounded the three-thousand camels and took them away. They also slew the guards!"* What a disaster! It was one catastrophe after another. His beloved servants and his livestock all vanished in a flash. His only hope was his children . . .

As his beloved children were gathered together enjoying themselves, a fierce storm suddenly blew up. The wind reduced the house to ruins! All ten children died. Not even one was left alive to comfort Job. This was no mere blow. It was a stab at his very soul. No more bad news followed after that. What more could have possibly happened?

Like a good father, he ran like lightning to the place where the house had stood. What an appalling sight! He could hear the cries and moans of his children! He saw their blood spilt, their bodies torn to pieces, arms, legs and heads cut off. Imagine how Job must have felt!

How did Job react, as utterly sickened as he was? He ripped his clothes, cut his hair and fell down and worshipped God, saying: *"I was born naked, naked shall I die. God gave, and now God has taken away. May His will be done. Blessed be the name of the Lord."*

Amazing! His pain (and what pain!) did not make him resentful and say: *"God, I did so many good things for You! And how have You repaid me? Instead of manna, now You give me gall? What harm have I ever done to You, anyway?"* Such thoughts did not even cross his mind.

His Wounds are Doubled

Job, who had once been extremely rich, was now extremely poor. Where he had once been the father of ten, he was now alone. Nobody ever had such a succession of great disasters. Nobody!

Just as he was beginning to get over his terrible misfortune, he was smitten with yet another disaster. He caught the dreaded disease of leprosy! He was cast completely out of society, since there was danger of spreading the disease. The former "tycoon" was now confined to a dunghill, as if he were a piece of rubbish. From the lowest point that he had already reached, he fell even further.

He was alone and naked, and where did he live—on a dunghill! In the heat of the summer, with his body covered with sores, Job suffered even more. The burning rays of the sun increased his misery. During the winter season with all the rain, the dunghill turned to mud. This was the new "home" for poor Job.

For food he had whatever people threw at him from a distance (that is, onto the dunghill!). How his body needed a little sleep! But no sooner did he doze off when he would awake from a terrible dream! Sleep, which he needed so badly, had now become a nightmare *(Job 7, 14)*.

Now that he had become such a wretched sight, everyone abandoned him: *"My friends have disappeared like a wave. They are like a mountain-torrent that has failed. Those who used to esteem me have now abandoned me" (Job 6, 15-16 LXX)*.

"I have implored my servant to come to me. I have shouted myself hoarse, but still he has not come. Everybody who looks at me is disgusted" (Job 19, 19 LXX). "Everybody mocks

me. Even the good-for-nothings" (Job 30, 1). *"They even spit on me"* (Job 30, 10). *"I have become a byword. Everyone gossips about me"* (Job 17, 6).

Previously, he had been famous throughout the world for his magnificence. Now, he was equally famous for his wretched plight.

The Taunts from his Friends

Two or three of his friends, kings from foreign lands, learned of his situation and decided to visit him. When they set eyes on him, they were thunderstruck! They did not speak for seven days, so great was the shock.

Once they recovered themselves, they began to talk to him. How Job needed to hear words of comfort. Indeed, it would have been better if they had said nothing at all! Their words were barbs in the wounds of their poor friend.

One of them said: *"Did you ever hear of any good man going through what has happened to you?"* (Job 4, 7). This was like telling him that if he'd been good, all this would not have happened. Another one said the same: *"It serves you right, all of this that has happened to you. You are paying for your sins!"*

Each of them spoke three times. Despite the pain he felt, Job found the strength to answer his friends. He tried to pour balm onto his own wounds. "*No,*" he insisted, "*you are wrong. After all, there are many people who are unrighteous and who still prosper*" *(cf. Job 21, 1-34).*

He tried desperately to find the reasons for his dreadful trials, but he was unable to do so. The Merciful Lord undertook to explain to Job the reason behind his terrible ordeal: "*I tested you for one reason only. So that your virtue, your faith and your patience would shine to the end.*"

"If an Olive isn't Pressed, it won't Produce Oil"

There is a story from the life of Saint Anthony the Great, where at one point the demons were physically beating him. He was literally black and blue from their blows. The great ascetic was almost in despair. He begged God to help him. When the demons left, the Lord finally appeared.

Saint Anthony asked God: "*Where were You, Lord? Why didn't You come right away and relieve my pain?*" The Lord replied, "*Anthony! I was with you all the time, and I have witnessed your great valor!*

Suppose you are righteous, yet you suffer unjustly. Know that you are suffering for the same reason as Job did—so that your virtue and valor will shine, and that your faith and patience will grow!

Whenever you are undergoing a spiritual trial or temptation, do you find yourself asking, "*God, where are You?*" Be assured that He is right beside you. He waits anxiously to see your faith, to see your valor and to see how truly you have committed yourself to the spiritual life in Christ.

Chapter Ten: David

"Do not touch my Anointed Ones" (Ps. 105, 15). It is as if the Lord is saying, through the mouth of the Prophet King David, *"Hands off those whom I have anointed!"* (that is, prophets, priests and kings). In those days, kings were anointed with oil by the high priests. They were the *"Lord's Anointed"*. Saul was king, having been anointed by the High Priest Samuel. King Saul was envious of David and threatened to slay him. Yet David behaved towards him as if he were his greatest benefactor!

The Wickedness Begins

The Philistines were the deadly enemies of the Jews. They were camped on the borders of Judah, ready to overtake it. Goliath the giant would often come out to taunt the Jews, saying to them: *"If any one of you dares, let him match himself against me. If he wins, we Philistines will become your servants" (1 Samuel 17, 9).* No one dared risk it, however, neither King Saul nor any of his men. Goliath challenged them for forty days. It became a matter of shame for the Israelites.

David was a simple shepherd boy, yet he took the bold decision to pit himself against

Goliath. *"You can not take on the Philistine,"* Saul told him, *"you are too young."* But David refused to listen. He fought against Goliath and . . . he beat him!

King Saul and the whole of Israel let out a huge sigh of relief. They had stopped the war. They were saved, thanks to the boldness of young David. A great feast was held in Judah. Women danced in the streets singing: *"Saul has defeated thousands, but David tens of thousands" (1 Samuel 18, 7).*

It was right and proper to hold the feast. It was right and proper for the women to hymn David. And yet, as right and natural as it was, it enraged Saul. From that time on, he sought to harm David! King Saul was infected with the poison of envy. From now on, he no longer acted according to reason, but according to *passion*.

The First Blows

David saw the hostile intentions of Saul. He saw how he now looked at him much differently and with an "evil eye". But David still tried to love him. Every day he played on his harp to entertain Saul in order to calm the king's spirits. On one occasion, while he was doing so, Saul threw a spear at him, with the intention of killing him. David nevertheless continued to try to entertain and calm him. Yet Saul struck a second time.

At that time the Law of Moses taught *"an eye for an eye, a tooth for a tooth . . ." (Ex. 21, 24)*. In other words, if someone puts your eye out, do not kill him, but its o. k. if you want to put one of his eyes out in return.[13] Here however, in this instance, David's life had been endangered. According to the Law, he therefore had the right, without incurring any legal guilt whatsoever, to kill Saul. Yet he still preferred to love, entertain and try to calm Saul, rather than kill him.

---

[13] Is it honorable or ethical, if somebody puts your eye out, to put out one of his in return? Certainly not! Why would God allow it? Saint John Chrysostom explains that the Jewish nation at that time was very vengeful and aggressive. They would kill somebody on the slightest pretext. So, in order to put a brake on murder, the Good Lord and Great Instructor allowed them to retaliate for what was done to them, but *only* that, no more. In other words, in order to forestall the worst (i. e., murder), He permitted the lesser evil. For example, did somebody cut your leg off? Do the same to him, but just don't kill him! Despite the fact that David grew up in such a bloodthirsty world, and despite the fact that God allowed retaliation for wrongs, he still behaved towards Saul as though he were his greatest benefactor. He did not even speak badly of him! Incredible, given the outlook of the time!

Finally, when he saw that Saul could not be calmed and that even his very presence annoyed the king, David did something else that was even more courageous. He went and ran far away from him, distancing himself from Saul with the hope that this would satisfy the wrath of his enemy. He left his home and went into exile, into a foreign and unknown land for the sake of his enemy! What a sacrifice! Note in particular that he did this, *not* for his brother or his friend, but for his *enemy*!

Still, there was no calming Saul, not even now that David was gone. He searched the cities, the villages, the mountains and the ravines in order to find David and to slay him!

A Most Critical Moment

David and his men went into a cave to rest from the manhunt launched by King Saul. Saul and his own troops also came into the same cave unaware that David was already there! Saul was exhausted and stretched out to sleep, as did his troops. David and his companions, who had been through a great deal for his sake, were still awake. It was a very critical moment indeed, and at the same time, a great opportunity for David.

His companions exerted the strongest pressure on him to kill Saul, and thus to finally be done with him. Here was his chance! They knew that David had the fear of God in him and so, to lure him on, they used the holy name of God. *"See," they said, "the day has come when the Lord has decided to deliver your enemy into your hands" (1 Samuel 24, 4).*

For a moment David was carried away and despite himself, he cut off an edge of Saul's cloak. Still, his conscience rebelled. He very quickly realized his mistake: *"God forbid that I ever do such a thing to Saul, my master, for he is the Lord's anointed" (1 Samuel 24, 6).* Not only this, but inside the cave, he struggled to convince his enraged companions not to kill Saul—and he succeeded!

Saul was asleep. He had no idea what was going on. He awoke, got ready and left the cave. David followed him. He called aloud to him: *"Lord King!"* Saul turned around. David fell to the ground and prostrated himself before him. It was as if he were saying: *"I remain your servant as before. You are still my king. Whatever you may do to me, you are still the Lord's anointed and therefore you deserve every respect."*

Like a good doctor, David tried to heal him. However, fearing that his efforts might not succeed, he said to Saul: *"Why do you listen to people when they say I am trying to kill you?" (1 Samuel 24, 9).*

According to Saint John Chrysostom, this was not in fact true. Ordinary people knew very well and could see for themselves the struggle David had undertaken for the salvation of Saul. He simply spoke to him like this to make his position easier and to make it sound as if Saul himself was somehow innocent and that others were the guilty ones. He wanted to initiate a dialogue with Saul. *(On Saul and David, Homily 2).*

"If I really wanted to kill you," said David, *"I would have done it today in the cave. But I didn't. I thought to myself: 'I will not stretch out my hand against my King, because he is the Lord's anointed.' See for yourself. The edge of your cloak is here in my hand. I cut it off. But I did not kill you. Yet you have taken an irrevocable decision to kill me. Whatever happens, my hand will not fall upon you."*

Saul listened. When David finished, he began to speak. He cried aloud: *"David, my son, is that your voice?" (1 Samuel 24, 16).* He broke down in tears. The miracle happened.

His cruel heart had shattered, only because of David's love.

Notice Saul's words, *"David, my son."* He now spoke to him with great tenderness and affection. He also asked, *"Is that your voice?"* Does this mean that he did not recognize David's voice?

Saint John Chrysostom teaches that, just as clouds can veil the beauty of the clear blue sky and make it seem different from what it is, so hostility clouds the face of people and make them seem other than what they are. When the clouds roll away, the beauty of the blue sky is revealed. When hostility is dispelled, we likewise see others as they really are. The same thing happened with Saul. His hatred (like dark clouds) would not allow him to listen to the voice of David. It seemed annoying and repulsive. Now that his passion had left him, he calmly recognized it *(On Saul and David, Homily 3).*

"You are better than me," continued Saul. *"You have been good to me, but I have abused you. You have told me what good you did to me today. God delivered me into your hand, but you did not slay me. The Lord will reward you. I know that you will one day*

become king![14] Swear that when you become king, you will not blot out my name from my family" (1 Samuel 24, 17-21). David promised this on oath and he kept his promise—and more besides—with his whole heart. This is what happened next.

Mephibosheth was the grandson of Saul, the son of Jonathon. Mephibosheth, however, was lame *(2 Samuel 4, 4).* David took him in and made him a member of the royal family. He lived permanently at the royal palace, even eating at the same table as King David. That's how foreign spite was to David!

Question 1: How did Saul know that David would become king? Saint John Chrysostom says that Saul realized that David had received God's help throughout this whole episode and that the time would come for the Lord to reward David *(On Saul and David, Homily 3).*

Question 2: How did humble David react to such a prophecy on the part of Saul? Did he take it as a joke or was he serious about it

---

[14] Just as the Good Lord justified and glorified Joseph, who had been despised and injured and made him Regent of Egypt, so He did the same for David who was also despised and hounded. Small in body but great in soul, David did indeed, become King of Israel!

from the start? He took it very seriously, as though it was already settled!

Question 3: Why such seriousness on the part of the humble David? He was so serious because the Lord had already informed him about what would happen. He had "inside information" that he would become Saul's successor.

The Death of Saul

King Saul was at war with the Philistines. He was being pursued by the enemy. They had killed his son Jonathan and now their spearmen aimed at Saul, wounding him under the ribs. He fell to the ground, bleeding and groaning in agony. There was a servant nearby. *"Finish me off,"* said Saul to the servant, *"so that the Philistines do not come and kill me and make a mockery of me."* The servant refused. Saul thus decided to commit suicide. The fatal act took place on Mount Gilboa *(1 Samuel 31, 1-8).*

At that time, David was a long way from Mount Gilboa, in the region of Ziklag. A man with torn clothes approached and prostrated himself before him. *"Where have you come from?"* asked David. *"From the Israelite camp. I have survived." "What happened in the battle?" "The Israelite army was routed. It fled.*

Many men were killed. King Saul was slain, as well as Jonathan, his son." "How do you know that Saul and his son were killed?" "I happened to be on Mount Gilboa. Suddenly I saw Saul leaning on his spear, wounded. As soon as he saw me, he begged me: 'Come here and kill me . . .' So I went up and killed him. I realized he wasn't going to live. I took the royal diadem he had on his head and the bracelet off his arm and I have brought them here to you my Lord!"[15] *"Where do you come from?" "I am the son of an Amalekite and I live in Judah." "How did you dare to raise your hand against the Lord's anointed?"* David gave orders that the man be killed! *"For the blood that you have spilled,"* said David, *"you are to blame, not me. I am having you killed because you yourself confessed that you killed Saul, the Lord's anointed" (2 Samuel 1, 1-16).*

Saul's death shattered David. He tore his clothes as an indication of his deep mourning. He smote his breast and wept bitterly. In regard to Mount Gilboa, which had received Saul when he had fallen, David said:

---

[15] This unknown man knew that Saul was David's enemy, but he did not know about David's lack of malice. In order to ingratiate himself with David and to win him over, he dressed up the tale in the telling.

"May neither dew nor rain ever fall upon it and may the fields never bear fruit." (2 Samuel 1, 21). And he went on: *"Daughters of Israel, lament also the passing of Saul."*

David also lamented the death of Jonathan, *"Jonathan, my brother, your death pains me. I loved you greatly."*

Conclusion

Let us recall that David slew the murderer of Saul, but did not kill Saul himself, who was persecuting him. Not only did he *not* murder him, he didn't even speak badly of him—and this at a time when murder was a daily occurrence. In the cave, where the great meeting took place, he called the man who had almost murdered him, *"My King and Lord"*. He even bowed down to him, because he was the *"Lord's anointed."*

Who was it who taught David to show such wonderful behavior to the *"Lord's anointed"*? It was God Himself! This means that no matter how corrupt the *"Lord's anointed"* might be, we have a sacred obligation not to speak badly about them, not to plot against them and to always respect them. This is true for our clergy, as well. In other words, they too must respect and honor the *"Lord's anointed."* The deacon must respect and revere all other deacons, priests and bishops. The priest must respect all other priests, deacons and bishops. The bishop must respect all other bishops, deacons and priests.

Just as the Lord, the Giver of Life, had mercy upon David and rewarded him, so He will have mercy upon and reward everyone—both lay people and clergy—who show the same respect to the *"Lord's anointed"*.

Chapter Eleven: Ruth

Ruth was known for her utter devotion to her mother-in-law. As the thread of her story unwinds, it is easy to see her great virtue. She lived more than a thousand years before Christ. Let's take a closer look at her story.

In those days, a severe famine afflicted the land of Israel. People were miserable. At that time, Elimelech and Naomi lived in Bethlehem with their two sons, Mahlon and Chilion. The famine forced the family into exile, into the land of Moab.

Elimelech died in Moab and thereafter his two sons took wives, Ruth and Orpah, from among the local women. Ten years passed and no children were born to them. Then suddenly something quite dreadful happened —both Mahlon and Chilion died! The widow Naomi remained abroad with her two daughters-in-law *(Ruth 1, 2-5).*

Naomi learned that the famine in Israel was over and decided to leave Moab and return to Bethlehem, to the house in which she had been born, to be with her friends and relations. What were her daughters-in-law supposed to do? Should they go with their mother-in-law or stay in their own country?

Their mothers, fathers and families were all in Moab. They didn't know a soul in Bethlehem. They must have said to themselves: *"Why should we go abroad and live in exile with our mother-in-law for the rest of our lives?"*

Apparently, these two virtuous daughters-in-law refused to entertain any such selfish idea. They thought it over and decided: *"Once we married, we didn't belong any more to our mothers or to our fathers, but only to our husbands. His homeland became our homeland. His mother became our mother. How then can we abandon our poor mother, a widow, when she is going through all this?"* These God-pleasing thoughts fell on fertile soil in their pure souls and bore fruit.

It's worth noting that both these daughters-in-law sacrificed their own interests for the sake of duty. They decided to live in exile, to leave their homes and to follow their mother-in-law and go and live in the place and house where their husbands had been born and where they had grown up and lived. So off they set, following Naomi, their mother-in-law.

In Naomi's case, a more egotistical and selfish woman would have thought: *"Thank goodness that both of my daughters-in-law are coming with me. I would have been alone, but they'll keep me company. How good they are!"* She would have done her best not to lose them. But Naomi did the exact opposite. She did everything in her power to persuade them to go back home.

Do you see? It wasn't only Ruth and Orpah who were generous souls; their mother-in-law was too. Naomi didn't think of her own interests, but she was thinking of what was best for her daughters-in-law. *"Please,"* she said to them, *"go back to your mothers. You have been so good to me and to my sons. I pray that God will be merciful towards you. May the Lord bless you and may you be happy with new husbands."* She showered them with kisses.

Naomi gave her daughters-in-law her blessing to return to their mothers and to make a new start in their lives. She gave them a golden opportunity to leave without feeling guilty.

When their mother-in-law made this noble suggestion, the two young women burst into tears. Both of them replied, crying with all their strength: *"No, we will go back with you to your people." "My daughters,"* insisted the mother-in-law, *"I beg you. Go back. Why do you want to come with me? Go back."* Again they started crying and wailing loudly. Finally, because of the overwhelming pressure that her mother-in-law brought to bear, Orpah give in. She kissed her mother-in-law many times and then went home.

The mother-in-law could have now been satisfied and thought: *"All right. That's not too bad. One is gone, the other has stayed."* But out of the goodness of her heart, she wanted everything to be arranged properly. She wanted to finish the good she had started to do. *"See,"* she said to Ruth, *"your sister-in-law's gone back. I beg you. Go along with her."*

Ruth might have answered: *"Well, since Orpah has left, I could go as well. In any case, my mother-in-law is very insistent."* But duty told her: *"Since your sister-in-law has left, that is all the more reason for you to stay, so that your poor husband's mother, who has become your own mother, will not be alone."* And that's what happened. Not only was Ruth unmoved by Orpah's withdrawal, but she became even more convinced and persistent.

She said to her mother-in-law: *"Don't pressure me! Where you go, I will go. Where you live, I will live. Where you die, I too will die. Where you will be buried, I will be buried.*

Nothing but death will separate me from you" (*Ruth 1, 15-18*). When Naomi realized that Ruth's decision was irreversible, she gave in.

They both set off for Bethlehem. Naomi was longing to see her friends and relations again, while Ruth was uneasy at the prospect of the unknown. They settled in Bethlehem and started their new life. Ruth never returned to her home in Moab. She died and was buried in Bethlehem.

People who are selfish and egocentric can not understand the fact that what gives meaning to life is being close to other people. Our responsibility and our duty towards others is what gives human life *true* meaning, not some kind of an "internal exile" within our own selves.

"I slept and dreamed that life was joy. I woke and saw that life was duty. I did my duty and joy came" (Tagore).

EPILOGUE

"God is wondrous in His saints."

We admire Abraham's obedience to God and his willingness to make a whole burnt offering of his only son, whom he loved so much! We admire the charity shown by Joseph and David.

Not only these examples, but many others as well are preserved and come alive for us in Holy Scripture. In other words, they are not simply "stories". They really happened to real people who believed in God—the God Who speaks to us in and through Holy Scripture.

Are there any similar circumstances that happened to people who believed in other "gods" or even in the "god" of science or philosophy? Certainly there are other stories outside of Holy Scripture that refer to similar cases of such wickedness, as is found in Cain, Saul and Joseph's brothers, as well as the rampant moral depravity as is found in the cities of Sodom and Gomorrah. There may also be other accounts outside of Holy Scripture that refer to somewhat similar virtues such as those which are found in Noah,

Abraham, Joseph, David, Ruth and the many other figures of Holy Scripture.

However, Holy Scripture is radically different from every other "religious" book. It is truly *the* "Book of God". The God Who speaks to us in and through Holy Scripture is not like the "gods" who speak in the books of other religions. He is the True God—the Triune God—the God who became man and united Himself to human nature in the Person of the Son of God, our Lord and Savior Jesus Christ.

All those who surrender to Him—to Christ the God-man—and who entrust themselves to the True God, will overcome all shortcomings and sufferings encountered in this life.

Not only this, but they will come to "live like the angels", forever progressing in their potential toward divine likeness (*Genesis 1, 26*).

They will live their lives with the hope of truly becoming, in the words of the Apostle Peter, "*partakers of divine nature*" (*2 Peter 1, 4*).

Indeed, *"God is wondrous in His saints."*